INTRODUCTION

HOW TO STUDY A PLAY

Studying on your own requires self-discipline and a carefully thought-out work plan in order to be effective.

- Drama is a special kind of writing (the technical term is 'genre') because it needs a performance in the theatre to arrive at a full interpretation of its meaning. Try to imagine that you are a member of the audience when reading the play. Think about how it could be presented on the stage, not just about the words on the page.
- Drama is always about conflict of some sort (which may be below the surface). Identify the conflicts in the play and you will be close to identifying the large ideas or themes which bind all the parts together.
- Make careful notes on themes, character, plot and any sub-plots of the play.
- Why do you like or dislike the characters in the play? How do your feelings towards them develop and change?
- Playwrights find non-realistic ways of allowing an audience to see into the minds and motives of their characters, for example, through an **aside** or music. Consider how such dramatic devices are used in the play you are studying.
- Think of the playwright writing the play. Why were these particular arrangements of events, characters and speeches chosen?
- Cite exact sources for all quotations, whether from the text itself or from critical commentaries. Wherever possible find your own examples from the play to back up your opinions.
- Where appropriate, comment in detail on the language of the passage you have quoted.
- Always express your ideas in your own words.

These York Notes offer an introduction to *The School for Scandal* and cannot substitute for close reading of the text and the study of secondary sources.

CHECK THE BOOK

Sheridan's 'Memorandum Book' from 1777, the year *The School for Scandal* was first produced, records the arrangements at the Drury Lane Theatre, from salaries to candles and clothing ('Stockings should be stamped with the Actors Name'). Sheridan's anxiety about his responsibility as Manager of about 175 staff is clear in his final comment: 'If with this plain Account before us we are inattentive or extravagant – shall we not deserve the Ruin which MUST follow?' cited in *Sheridan: Comedies,* ed. by Peter Davidson (Palgrave Macmillan, 1986, pp. 33–4).

CHECK THE BOOK

Chapter 7 of Linda Kelly's *Richard Brinsley Sheridan: A Life* (Sinclair-Stevenson, 1997) has an account of the triumphant first night of *The School for Scandal* that emphasises the importance of Sheridan's well-chosen cast.

CONTEXT

Dr Parr, one of Sheridan's teachers at Harrow, recalled: 'He was mischievous enough, but his pranks were accompanied by a sort of vivacity and cheerfulness, which delighted Sumner [the Headmaster] and myself.' (Letter from Dr Parr to Sheridan's biographer, Thomas Moore, cited in Kelly, *Richard Brinsley Sheridan: A Life*, p. 21).

READING *THE SCHOOL FOR SCANDAL*

> Whatever Sheridan has done or has chosen to do has been, par excellence, always the best of its kind. He has written the best comedy (*School for Scandal*) the best drama [*The Duenna*], ... the best farce – (*the Critic* – it is only too good for a farce), and the best Address (Monologue on Garrick), and, to crown all, delivered the very best Oration (the famous Begum Speech) ever conceived or heard in this country.
>
> Byron, *Journals*, 17 and 18 December 1813

By the time he wrote *The School for Scandal* in 1777, Richard Brinsley Sheridan had already scored notable successes on the London stage, written a popular opera and become manager of London's most famous theatre. He had also, sensationally, run away with and then married the most famous – and beautiful – young singer of the time and fought two duels with a rival, in the second of which he was seriously injured. All this he achieved without the benefit of wealth, noble birth or education beyond an undistinguished few years at Harrow School, and at the relatively tender age of twenty-five. Sheridan had also yet to embark upon a second and even more daring venture for the son of an Irish actor-manager – his dazzling political career as a leading Member of Parliament.

The author of *The School for Scandal* was born in Dublin in 1751, the second son of Thomas Sheridan, actor and manager of Smock Alley Theatre, and Frances Sheridan, who achieved some fame herself as a novelist and playwright. When his father was forced to leave Dublin in 1754 after a riot destroyed his theatre, Richard and his sister were left behind and only joined their parents in England when he was eight. Despite his considerable talents and reputation as an actor, manager and teacher of elocution, Thomas Sheridan was burdened by debts and eventually moved to France, leaving Richard behind at Harrow School, where he was tormented by the boys as 'a poor player's son'. His mother died in France in 1766. While his father taught him grammar and oratory, Richard's education also included Latin, mathematics and swordsmanship (training that proved most useful later). His father intended him to become a lawyer but Richard was determined to make his living as a writer.

Sheridan's personal life became public drama when he eloped from Bath with the famous singer Elizabeth Linley in 1772. She was fleeing the unwelcome attentions of Captain Thomas Mathews, an older, married man, and Richard had promised to escort her to safety in a convent in France. He declared his love for her on the way and they underwent a form of marriage near Calais. On their return to England, Sheridan responded to insults from Mathews by challenging him to a duel, which he won. A second duel with Mathews was more serious: Sheridan was gravely injured. He recovered, married Elizabeth officially in 1773 and decided that he would support them both by his writing.

Within two years Sheridan was rewarded with success. 1775 saw the production at Covent Garden of *The Rivals*, *St Patrick's Day* and his comic opera, *The Duenna* (with music by the Linleys, his wife's family). Although the first night of *The Rivals* was a failure, Sheridan's revisions ensured that subsequent performances were greeted with acclaim. The next year he succeeded David Garrick as manager of the Theatre Royal, Drury Lane. In 1777 he adapted Vanbrugh's *The Relapse* as *A Trip to Scarborough* and, on 8 May, achieved his greatest triumph with the opening night of *The School for Scandal*. The leaders of fashionable society filled the audience and were delighted with the production; such was the roar of applause at the falling of the screen in Act IV that a passer-by thought the theatre was collapsing. After the final curtain Sheridan went on the town, telling Byron later that 'he was knocked down and put into the watch-house for making a row in the streets and for being found intoxicated by the watchmen' (cited in Kelly, *Richard Brinsley Sheridan: A Life*, p. 77).

Although he continued to be involved with Drury Lane until 1809, Sheridan's attention now turned to politics. He was elected to the House of Commons as MP for Stafford in 1780 and was active throughout the turbulent years of the French Revolution, war with France and the Regency crisis. His fame as an orator was enormous; when he spoke at the trial of Warren Hastings for abuses in India,

WWW. CHECK THE NET

The Sheridan website by David Taylor at **http://people.pwf.cam.ac.uk/dft21** has information on his life and works, extracts from speeches and a gallery of cartoons by the famous caricaturist Gillray featuring Sheridan at various stages in his political career.

CONTEXT

Eighteenth-century theatres were unruly places. The audience was noisy and made their reactions clear by hissing, laughing or, at times, crying. Audience displeasure could turn to violence: Drury Lane was wrecked by riots five times between 1743 and 1776.

CHECK THE BOOK
There is a good description of London theatres in Sheridan's time in Chapter 12 of Fintan O'Toole's biography, *A Traitor's Kiss* (Granta Books, 1997).

crowds queued for hours and paid up to fifty guineas for a ticket. He wrote only one other major play, the historical drama *Pizarro* in 1799; although a great success at the time, it is today forgotten. Staunchly independent, Sheridan was a supporter of liberal causes, including the abolition of slavery and political and religious freedom in Ireland. His independence meant that whilst he held some government posts and was the unofficial leader of the Whigs after the death of Fox, he was never rewarded with high office. Despite his successes in the theatre he was almost permanently short of money and when he lost his seat in 1812 his creditors closed in. He had the humiliation of having to spend some periods in sponging-houses – debtors' prisons – until money could be raised to release him. Eventually, like Charles in *The School for Scandal*, he was forced to sell off his possessions, including Joshua Reynolds' famous portrait of his first wife, Eliza, as St Cecilia. He died in July 1816 at the age of sixty-five, with bailiffs at the door. In a final reversal of fortune, he was buried in Poets' Corner in Westminster Abbey amid much pomp and with aristocratic pallbearers.

The School for Scandal has remained popular ever since its first production because the brilliance of its dialogue is combined with sharp characterisation, **satire** and a measure of **sentiment**. Though recent critics have tended to prefer the more caustic comedy of the Restoration period and questioned the realism of the reconciliations at the end of the play, actors have continued to delight in Sheridan's wit and command of comic situations. The play has been a favourite vehicle for famous actors; in 1949 Laurence Olivier wrote of the 'play's life and spirit pulsating through his body and soul', declaring 'this play will never grow old' (cited in Kelly, *Richard Brinsley Sheridan: A Life*, p. 81). Bernard Shaw praised how the language imposes its own rhythm, almost like an opera, in ways that come naturally to a practised actor, and the modern writer and translator Ranjit Bolt has described Sheridan as 'a major genius'.

Sheridan was himself aware of his place in theatrical history. He borrowed much from earlier writers such as Wycherley and Congreve, softening the shaper edges of the satire for an age becoming more interested in sentiment, a term which is, at the same time, subject to some mockery in the play: the villain, Joseph

Surface, is **ironically** dubbed 'a man of sentiment'. Although Sheridan criticised sentimentality, he brings his two couples together at the end of the play and this romantic aspect appealed to nineteenth century audiences. As a theatrical manager as well as a playwright, Sheridan understood the importance of attracting a large and regular audience. During his time at Drury Lane the theatre was enlarged to accommodate a growing middle-class audience: when he took over the theatre in 1776 it had 2,300 seats; after the rebuilding in 1794 it could accommodate 3,611. Following closely on the success of *She Stoops to Conquer* by fellow Irishman Oliver Goldsmith, *The Rivals* and *The School for Scandal* are the only plays by Sheridan that are still regularly performed today, though his short **burlesque** *The Critic* (1779) is occasionally revived. Sheridan's sparkling dialogue and satirical treatment of society link him with Oscar Wilde, an Irishman writing a hundred years later.

CONTEXT

Theatre audiences in Sheridan's time were large: compare the 3,611 capacity at Drury Lane with the capacity of today's National Theatre main Olivier stage in London, which is only 1,160. Spectators were a cross-section of London society, from labourers and servants in the upper gallery to the gentry in the boxes.

The play is firmly rooted in its time, where a relatively small social circle eagerly devours reputations and recycles scandal. Sheridan knew for himself the power of rumour and importance of honour. His own two duels were in part occasioned by notices in the newspapers – reputation could literally be a matter of life and death. In order to be accepted within the circle of the 'scandalous college' as a newly-arrived county girl, Lady Teazle needs to participate in its gossip – she is cursed by Lady Sneerwell when she renounces its practices at the end of the play. Here too Sheridan was drawing on his own experience; he was mocked at school for being the son of an actor and desperately wished to enter polite society even though his background would seem to deny any possibility of this. The financial success of the play (it earned £15,000 in its first two seasons) enabled him to enter politics, and it was for his parliamentary career that he wished to be remembered. He would have been disappointed that he was buried with the poets rather than the statesmen in Westminster Abbey, remarkable though any such fame would have seemed to his impoverished parents.

The public thirst for gossip and our delight in the exposure of hypocrisy are, of course, as strong today as in Sheridan's time – perhaps even more so. For a student of the play much can be gained

CHECK THE NET

Portraits and cartoons of Sheridan can be found on the National Portrait Gallery site: **www.npg.org.uk**. Click 'search the collection' and search for 'Sheridan' as sitter. Check carefully – there is another, more modern, Richard Brinsley Sheridan in the collection!

from understanding the context and the language of the play. However, its central concerns seem as relevant today as they did two hundred years ago and they continue to fascinate us. We enjoy both the barbed comments of the scandalmongers and the prospect of their downfall; the hypocritical Joseph Surface is the kind of stage villain we delight in watching, however much we may profess to despise his methods. Although Sheridan wrote the play with the skills of specific actors in mind, his skill with dialogue has ensured its popularity ever since. Modern productions may be more interested in 'the itch beneath the powder', as Tyrone Guthrie put it (cited in Gyles Brandreth, *John Gielgud: An Actor's Life*, Sutton Publishing, 2000, p. 68), and attempt to reveal moral **ambiguity** in the text or stress the grubby reality under the polished surface of the lives of the gentry. Certainly money seems almost as important as reputation, from Charles' large debts to Lady Teazle's request for £200, from Sir Oliver's vast riches earned as a 'Nabob' in India to the servant Trip's attempt to raise a loan of £20. Understanding Sheridan's craft and appreciating the context, as well as thinking about the issues raised, should help you not only succeed in your studies but also enjoy the play.

PART TWO

THE TEXT

NOTE ON THE TEXT

The School for Scandal was first performed on 8 May 1777 at the Drury Lane theatre where Sheridan had become manager a year earlier. It was an immediate success, running for twenty nights and a further forty-five performances in the next season. Until the end of the century it was performed more than any other play in London. As well as contemporary versions in German and French it was translated into Russian at the command of the Empress Catherine the Great and performed at the coming of age of her grandson and successor Alexander I. It also acquired classic status in the United States, where it was said to be George Washington's favourite play.

The text of *The School for Scandal* exists in various forms, for despite its popularity Sheridan did not allow it to be printed during his lifetime. This may be because, like Sir Benjamin, he believed ''tis very vulgar to print' (I.1.254) – or it may have been a way of protecting an extremely valuable investment. Both European translations and American editions were based on pirated versions compiled by actors or from unofficial copies of a draft. Sheridan was also an inveterate reviser of his own works – indeed, his other famous comedy, *The Rivals*, had a lukewarm reception at its first performance and only achieved success after extensive cuts and revisions. The various refinements and alterations can be found detailed in scholarly editions such as the New Mermaids edition on which these Notes are based. If you use another edition, or even an online version of the text, you should be aware that whilst the changes may not be of major significance they can sometimes surprise you.

These Notes are based on the New Mermaids edition of the play, edited by Ann Blake (A & C Black, third edition, 2004). All line numbers refer to this edition.

WWW. CHECK THE NET

There are online versions of *The School for Scandal* on Project Gutenberg (**www.gutenberg.org**) and on Bartleby, where the play is displayed in scenes (**www.bartleby.com**). The Project Gutenberg version warns readers that it 'differs in many respects from that which is generally known', including the introduction of Miss Verjuice (in place of Snake) in Act I Scene 1.

SYNOPSIS

CONTEXT

Such was the fame of *The School for Scandal* that his enemies often later referred to Sheridan in terms of characters from the play. In 1789, when he was an influential political figure, *The Times* attacked Sheridan by referring to 'the false and scurrilous paragraphs with which the Opposition prints [newspapers] are daily furnished by Mr Surface and his would-be witty associates.' In 1804, a scurrilous reference to Sheridan claimed that in the play 'he drew from himself both the profligacy of *Charles* and the hypocrisy of *Joseph*' (cited in O'Toole, *A Traitor's Kiss*, pp. 245, 413).

Although Sheridan's plot involves a number of disguises, rumours and deceptions, the story is in essence simple. It concerns a test of the true virtue of two brothers: the elder a smooth hypocrite, the younger a reckless but generous spendthrift. Their wealthy uncle uncovers their true natures and the younger brother is rewarded with fortune and happiness in love. In an important subsidiary action, an older man is reconciled with his lively young wife to provide a second happy couple at the final curtain.

The events of the play concern members of London's fashionable society and take place in the houses of Lady Sneerwell, Sir Peter Teazle and of two brothers, Joseph and Charles Surface. Following the death of their father, the brothers have been supported by their wealthy uncle, Sir Oliver Surface, who has been in India for fifteen years. Sir Peter, their uncle's friend, acted as a kind of guardian to the boys whilst they grew up. Joseph, the elder brother, is known as a 'man of sentiment' for the moral tone of his conversation; he is the favourite of Sir Peter who wishes him to marry his ward Maria. Maria, however, is in love with the younger brother, Charles, though at her guardian's insistence she has cut off all contact with him because of his extravagance, which has left him deeply in debt. Sir Peter has recently married a much younger woman and brought her from the country to London, where she has joined the group of scandalmongers led by Lady Sneerwell.

The play opens with Lady Sneerwell, a widow, plotting to spread rumours in the newspapers with her servant, Snake. Although it is widely believed that she is interested in Joseph, she reveals that she is actually in love with his younger brother Charles. Her circle of scandalmongers arrives and they share the latest malicious gossip. We then meet Sir Peter, whose marriage is being made miserable by quarrels. He is also angry that Maria is resisting his plan for her to marry Joseph. Rowley, his faithful retainer, tells him that Sir Oliver has unexpectedly returned from India. After a demonstration of the tempestuous relationship between Sir Peter and Lady Teazle as they quarrel over her extravagance, the scene moves back to Lady

Sneerwell's house. Left alone with Maria, Joseph declares he loves her but is interrupted by Lady Teazle, who had believed Joseph was her admirer. Joseph manages to persuade Lady Teazle he was merely attempting to stop Maria telling Sir Peter about his feelings for Lady Teazle. Sir Peter's next meeting with his wife appears to promise reconciliation but later they quarrel so bitterly he talks of a separation or divorce.

Sir Oliver expresses his unwillingness to take the reputations of his nephews at face value. Instead, he has decided to visit them in disguise in order to test their true characters. He first calls on Charles in the company of Moses, pretending to be Mr Premium, a moneylender. The audience is given a glimpse of Charles at home, drinking and singing in praise of women with his friends, before Sir Oliver and Moses arrive. Discovering that Charles has sold almost everything of value, Sir Oliver agrees to buy the family portraits. Although initially disgusted at his nephew's reckless disposal of the family history, his uncle is won over when Charles refuses to sell one picture, even when offered a large sum – it is the picture of Sir Oliver himself. Charles promptly gives Rowley some of the money to take to Mr Stanley, a poor relation.

The climax of the play occurs in Joseph's library, where he plans to seduce Lady Teazle. When they are interrupted by Sir Peter, Lady Teazle hides behind a screen. Here she overhears her husband tell Joseph that he suspects she has been unfaithful to him with Charles. Instead of condemning her, he says he is prepared to give her a generous settlement so they can live apart in peace. Charles arrives and Sir Peter in turn hides to eavesdrop. Charles denies any wrongdoing with Lady Teazle and is on the point of incriminating his brother when Joseph reveals that Sir Peter has been listening to everything. Charles drags Sir Peter out of hiding and, after Joseph departs, Sir Peter tells Charles that Joseph is also hiding a woman in the room. Charles knocks down the screen to reveal Lady Teazle who, moved by her husband's generosity, refuses to join Joseph in lying about their affair and confesses her shame. Shortly afterwards Sir Oliver calls on Joseph in the guise of the impoverished Mr Stanley. When Joseph offers empty words and no practical help, Sir Oliver's decision to make Charles his heir is confirmed.

QUESTION

'A plot summary of *The School for Scandal* is more misleading than summaries of plots usually are, for it will of necessity focus on the conventional and contrived – and "sentimental" – aspects of the play' (John Loftis, *Sheridan and the Drama of Georgian England*, Blackwell, 1977, p. 87). How far do you agree with this statement?

The scandalmongers hurry to Sir Peter's as rumours of the scene at Joseph's house begin to spread. Sir Peter drives them out in fury and goes to seek reconciliation with his wife. Sir Oliver reveals himself to his nephews and all denounce Joseph. Although Lady Sneerwell and Joseph attempt one last deception to discredit Charles and Lady Teazle, they fail since Snake, their agent, has been paid more to tell the truth. Charles is reunited with Maria and they will be married the next morning.

DETAILED SUMMARIES

PROLOGUE

- The actor playing Sir Peter Teazle introduces the theme of scandal.

The actor playing Sir Peter Teazle – in the first production, Thomas King – points out that we don't need to be taught how to gossip. Mimicking an imaginary Lady Wormwood, sipping tea and enjoying the latest scandal in the papers, he wonders whether the playwright can have any success in his campaign against scandal.

COMMENTARY

Although presumably already in costume as Sir Peter, the actor addresses the audience directly – possibly standing in front of the curtain. The Prologue and Epilogue were conventional theatrical devices of the time and, as was customary, were written by others as vehicles for leading actors. They put a frame around the play, marking a transition from the world of the audience to the world depicted on the stage – but reminding the audience that the events on stage reflect their own lives (and, by implication, their own failings too). A skilful actor is also presented with the opportunity for a little comic business. Sir Peter mimics 'Lady Wormwood' sipping tea and savouring the scandal in the paper – until she realises she is herself the victim and flings the paper 'behind the fire' (line 25). The satirical tone of the play is made clear from the start.

CONTEXT

David Garrick (1717–79), who wrote the Prologue, was a famous actor and playwright, and Sheridan's predecessor as manager of the Theatre Royal, Drury Lane. In the first production Sir Peter was played by Thomas King (1730–1805), a leading comic actor and author of several **farces**.

CONTEXT

The line, **'our young bard'** (line 29), refers to the fact that Sheridan was only twenty-five when *The School for Scandal* was first performed.

The conventional rhyming couplets contrast with Sheridan's more naturalistic (though still carefully crafted) prose. The final words are also a reminder that all has been devised to gain our approval, just as the Chorus in Shakespeare's *Henry V* asks the audience 'gently to hear, kindly to judge, our play' (*Henry V*, Prologue, line 34).

CONTEXT

Comic business is the term for an actor or actors taking an opportunity to play an incident for laughter, perhaps introducing additional activity on stage. Here the actor, dressed as the elderly Sir Peter, is pretending to be an elegant lady, with exaggerated speech and actions. At the end of Act I Scene 1, the stage directions make it clear that two of the actors exit and return up to six times in a few lines, a chance for further comic antics.

GLOSSARY

5	**vapours** fainting
8	***quantum sufficit*** a sufficient amount
15	***sal volatile*** smelling salts (to combat 'the vapours')
18	**poz** positively
24	**Wormwood** a bitter plant
36	**Don Quixote** the eponymous Spanish knight ('cavalliero', line 40) in Cervantes' tale, famed for his deluded acts of chivalry
38	**hydra** many-headed monster

ACT I

SCENE 1

- Lady Sneerwell and Snake are seen plotting their latest scandalmongering.
- Joseph Surface brings news of his brother Charles' extravagance.
- Maria enters, fleeing her unwelcome suitor, Sir Benjamin Backbite, and his uncle.
- Mrs Candour, Crabtree and Sir Benjamin Backbite arrive and the gossiping intensifies until Maria, upset by their malicious speculation about Charles, leaves in distress.

As the curtain rises on Lady Sneerwell's house, Lady Sneerwell (a wealthy widow) and Snake (whom she employs to spread rumours) are discovered at her dressing table, drinking chocolate

CONTEXT

In Sheridan's theatre, the curtain would rise at the opening of Act I and not be lowered again until the end of the play. Scene changes were indicated by moving 'flats' at either side of the stage and lowering or raising 'drop cloths'. See **Literary background: Theatre in the late eighteenth century**.

CONTEXT

The *Town and Country Magazine* (line 17) and the *Morning Post* were new publications at the time Sheridan was writing, with regular columns of gossip and scandal; names were suggested by initials rather than being spelt in full (see the example in the Prologue, lines 14–16).

and discussing the scandal they have spread by word of mouth and in the papers. Contrary to appearances, Lady Sneerwell reveals she has no interest in Joseph Surface but, despite herself, loves his profligate younger brother Charles. She therefore wishes to destroy the relationship between Charles and Maria (Sir Peter Teazle's ward), whilst Joseph himself wishes to marry Maria ('or her fortune', line 58). It is clear it is her money that he is after.

Joseph enters and confirms that his brother Charles is close to ruin as a result of extravagance. Once Snake leaves, Joseph expresses doubts about his loyalty to them. At this point Maria enters unannounced, fleeing the unwelcome attentions of her 'disagreeable lover' Sir Benjamin Backbite and his 'odious' Uncle Crabtree (lines 131–3). She particularly resents their malicious gossip. Just as Maria has described scandal as 'contemptible' (line 158), Mrs Candour is announced, followed soon after by Crabtree and Sir Benjamin Backbite. With the 'school for scandal' now assembled, they proceed to savour the latest gossip. Their relish in the details of Charles' financial troubles finally becomes too much for Maria, who leaves in distress. Lady Sneerwell and Joseph are the last to leave, she to 'plot mischief', he to 'study sentiments' (lines 365–6) – that is, to practise some of the fine-sounding sayings that so impress Sir Peter Teazle.

Commentary

This long scene (only the 'screen scene', Act IV Scene 3, has more lines) sets the plot in motion, establishes the comic tone and introduces the main characters. By the end of the scene, the audience may be expecting a romantic plot to unfold, with Lady Sneerwell and Maria as rivals for Charles (though neither dare show their affection in public), complicated by Joseph's apparent interest in Lady Sneerwell and the financial ruin facing Charles. The play begins with a note of intrigue and soon the witty dialogue and often ridiculous characters establish the tone.

Sheridan regularly alerts us to key aspects of a character before they appear: Lady Sneerwell tells Snake that Joseph is 'artful, selfish, and malicious' in line 72 ahead of his arrival on stage, while the fact that Sir Peter admires him suggests the older man is gullible long before his first appearance in Act I Scene 2. Charles is described as 'that libertine, that extravagant, that bankrupt in fortune and reputation' as early as lines 65–6, though he does not appear on stage until Act III Scene 3. The names of some of the characters also make Sheridan's purposes clear: the audience will expect Lady Sneerwell and Sir Benjamin Backbite to be **satirical** creations with a distinctive but narrow range of behaviour. Yet we also observe the tensions that some, at least, of the characters feel: Lady Sneerwell, despite her obvious delight in causing suffering to others (see lines 30–1), confesses she would 'sacrifice everything' for Charles (line 68). Although she arrives at Lady Sneerwell's in search of refuge, Maria's distaste at the 'mischief' (line 169) caused by scandal finally forces her to flee the school's company just as she fled from Sir Benjamin. Joseph is established as a hypocrite from the start, 'a sentimental knave' in Lady Sneerwell's words (line 73). He seems to agree with Maria about the 'mischief' of gossip (lines 150–1) and yet a few lines later he supports Lady Sneerwell by saying that 'conversation where the spirit of raillery is suppressed will ever appear tedious and insipid' (lines 155–6). In each case his language is sufficiently convoluted to give the appearance of virtue, though the careful listener will realise that it is not possible to condemn 'the jest which plants a thorn' and at the same time approve of 'the spirit of raillery', which is the same thing. Through these tensions, Sheridan achieves a degree of depth in his principal characters, which would not otherwise be there. Indeed, Joseph's villainy is all the more fascinating for his duplicity and the audience may expect the satisfaction of Joseph's unmasking by the end of the play.

On stage, the atmosphere of intrigue is established by the setting. Lady Sneerwell and Snake are at her dressing table, drinking chocolate – an intimate, conspiratorial scene. They refer to a number of scandals which confirm the emphasis on gossip and, more widely, on social reputation. They also draw attention to Lady Sneerwell's central role in 'reducing others to the level of my own injured reputation' (line 34), adding a hint of vulnerability to her malicious character. A period of busy comings and goings follows as at various points additional characters are announced – the first is Joseph, whose hypocrisy Snake has described and which is rapidly confirmed by his own words. In turn, Joseph denounces Snake for

QUESTION

What do you notice about Sheridan's use of names? Is the effect the same in each case? See the **Extended commentary** on the first part of this scene for some suggestions.

CHECK THE BOOK

Critic John Loftis draws attention to similarities between *The School for Scandal* and Arthur Murphy's (1727–1605) *Know Your Own Mind,* first performed just three months before Sheridan's play and also exposing the intrigues and hypocrisies of London society. 'To Murphy as to Sheridan "sentiment" and "sensibility" were the cant terms of hypocrites, the verbal camouflage of malice' (*Sheridan and the Drama of Georgian England,* pp. 94–5).

> **QUESTION**
> How does Sheridan vary the pace and maintain interest in this long scene?

becoming familiar with Sir Peter's loyal servant Rowley (lines 123–5), a hint that is realised when in Act V Scene 3, Snake tells Lady Sneerwell that he has 'been offered double to speak the truth' (line 181). Mrs Candour, true to her name, slanders by her 'very gross affectation of good nature and benevolence' (line 168), as Maria says. Like Sir Benjamin and Crabtree, Mrs Candour is a much more two-dimensional character than Lady Sneerwell or Joseph. Similarly, perhaps constrained by having an inexperienced actor for her part (see the **Detailed summary** for **Act V Scene 3**), Sheridan gives Maria quite a passive role. This may also reflect the fact that he already has a strong female lead in Lady Teazle, who will play a significant part in the defeat of Joseph and Lady Sneerwell as well as providing a spirited opponent for Sir Peter.

Sheridan demonstrates much skill in allowing these characters to condemn themselves out of their own mouths, making for a lively set piece that is hugely enjoyable to watch. The tone changes briefly, however, when the topic turns to Charles Surface. Here Maria's discomfort breaks through the brittle surface to remind us of the hurt that scandal can cause. The scene ends on a lighter note as Sir Benjamin and Crabtree, on the point of leaving, cannot resist returning on the point of their exits to complete 'a subject they have not quite run down' (lines 358–9) – the stage direction '*Going*' or '*Going*' and '*Returns*' occurs up to six times in some manuscripts, indicating comic actions on stage by these two characters.

See **Extended commentaries – Text 1** for a more detailed analysis of the first part of this scene.

GLOSSARY

1	**paragraphs** scandalous gossip in the newspapers
4	**intrigue** secret love affair
17	***tête-à-tête*** a private conversation, here it is the name of the scandal column in the *Town and Country Magazine*
46	**ward** a person (in this case Maria) under the protection of another (i.e. Sir Peter) – not to be confused with another meaning of ward, in line 324, where it means an electoral district

48	**City knight** a London merchant who had been knighted
48	**jointure** the bequest a husband promises his wife at the time of marriage
55	**intercourse** dealings (sexual intercourse is not implied, as Lady Sneerwell makes clear)
65	**libertine** a person, usually a man, who does not obey conventional morality
73	**sentimental** showing refined feelings or moral reflections (not the modern sense of being excessively emotional), used **ironically** here
87	**arraigning** calling to account
91	**sensibility** sensitivity, especially to moral or emotional feelings
99	**distresses** legal term for the seizure of goods to pay a debt
100	**execution** another legal term: the carrying out of a court order to seize a debtor's goods
131	**lover** here Maria means nothing more than 'admirer'
156	**raillery** banter, mockery
179	**the town** London's fashionable society
197	**diligence** a stagecoach
213	**dropsy** swelling (a medical condition, though Mrs Candour implies pregnancy)
216	**house of no extraordinary fame** place of ill repute, i.e. a brothel
243	**rebus** a kind of riddle in which pictures, symbols or letters are used to represent words or syllables in order to form a message or phrase
247	**conversazione** private gathering for music and conversation
255	**lampoons** mockery in the form of **satirical** prose or verse
261	**Petrarch's Laura** the beloved addressed in the poetry of the fourteenth-century Italian poet Petrarch (1304–74)
261–2	**Waller's Sacharissa** the lady addressed in the smooth verses of the seventeenth-century poet Edmund Waller (1606–87) ('Sacharissa' implies her sweetness)
273–4	**wedding livery** uniforms for the servants to wear at the ceremony
275	**pressing** urgent (with a sexual implication)

continued

CONTEXT

The phrase, 'measure swords' (lines 217–16), is a reference to duelling, which had undergone a revival towards the end of the eighteenth century. Sheridan himself was an accomplished swordsman and fought two duels (see **Reading *The School for Scandal***). His play *The Rivals* includes two threatened duels, though they are brought to comic resolution without blows being struck.

CONTEXT

Sir Oliver has made his fortune during fifteen years in India (line 315), which at this time was largely in the control of the East India Company, a commercial organisation with monopoly powers of trade with India. It effectively governed the country and its British employees were nicknamed 'nabobs' (derived from the Urdu word for ruler, 'nawab') because of the great wealth they often acquired. In the play no comment is made on the dubious origins of this money, though later Sheridan was one of the prime movers to impeach and then try Warren Hastings, the Governor-General, for abuses of his power over the Indian population.

287	**valetudinarians** people suffering from long-term or chronic illness
315	**East Indies** at this time, the phrase included the Indian subcontinent
323	**the Jews** Sir Benjamin here means moneylenders, reflecting a contemporary stereotype
324	**Old Jewry** Old Jewry Street lay at the heart of the old Jewish district in London
324–5	**ward … alderman** an alderman was a senior member of the city council chosen by other councillors rather than elected by a ward or district, so Crabtree is being theatrical rather than strictly accurate
327	**tontine** a form of lottery in which several subscribers share a common fund, with their benefits increasing as members die
331	**securities** people who have promised to guarantee his loans
332	**officer** bailiff
353	**wainscots** wooden panelling on the interior walls of a house
362	**I doubt** I fear
366	**sentiments** moral sayings, especially fine-sounding ones

SCENE 2

- Sir Peter Teazle reveals that his marriage to a young wife is marred by quarrels.
- He tells his servant Rowley of his frustration that Maria refuses to marry Joseph Surface.
- Rowley disagrees with St Peter's preference for Joseph over his younger brother Charles.
- We learn that Sir Oliver has returned unexpectedly early from India.

The scene moves to Sir Peter Teazle's house. Addressing the audience directly, Sir Peter describes the trials of 'an old bachelor [who] marries a young wife' (line 1). Although he married her as a country girl, six months in London have given Lady Teazle extravagant tastes and Sir Peter is mocked in society for his naivety. Despite all this, he confesses, he still loves her. In conversation with Rowley, his faithful servant, he blames his quarrels with his wife on Lady Teazle and on the malicious influence of Lady Sneerwell and her set. To make matters worse, his ward Maria rejects his choice of Joseph Surface as her husband. Sir Peter is sure this is because she intends instead to marry his extravagant younger brother, Charles. Whilst Rowley defends Charles, Sir Peter praises Joseph as 'a Man of Sentiment' (lines 52–3).

Rowley informs Sir Peter that Sir Oliver, whose generosity has given his nephews Joseph and Charles their financial independence, has returned unexpectedly early from India. He intends to put the brothers to the test. Sir Peter makes Rowley promise to keep secret the troubles between himself and Lady Teazle.

COMMENTARY

Sir Peter's honesty and openness is an immediate contrast to the atmosphere of intrigue in the play's opening scene. He is alone on stage and shares his unhappiness with the audience. We are amused at his blindness to his own weaknesses even if we may also warm to him as a much more genuine character than the scandalmongers we have just observed. Sheridan presents a neat balance in Sir Peter's language and his feelings: 'Lady Teazle made me the happiest of men – and I have been the miserablest dog' (lines 2–3). He loves his young wife – yet he'll 'never be weak enough to own it' (line 17). He even says in line 25 that he would be pleased to hear of her death – though we have already heard enough not to believe everything he tells Rowley. Would the 'sweetest-tempered man' that Sir Peter claims to be, complain to his wife that he hates her teasing 'a hundred times a day' (line 30)?

Just as Sir Peter's openness contrasts with the cruelty of Lady Sneerwell's set, Rowley's honesty is very different from Snake's guile. His faith in Charles indicates that we may expect the younger

CHECK THE BOOK

The figure of an older husband troubled by a young wife was a stock character in Restoration and eighteenth century plays such as Congreve's (1670–1729) *The Old Bachelor* (1693) revived at Drury Lane in 1776 and Wycherley's (1640–1716), *The County Wife* (1673). In Wycherley's play a young wife brought to London falls for the seductions of the city (more literally than in Lady Teazle's case) while her fashionable friends are more concerned with the outward show of 'honour' (that is, social reputation) than with genuine morality.

brother to be very different from the elder, despite Sir Peter's praise of the 'man of sentiment'. We have already learnt in the previous scene that Joseph's sentiments are a sham, so we see the **irony** in Sir Peter's claim that he 'acts up to the sentiments he professes' (line 53) – Joseph is indeed only acting when he pretends to virtue, as we shall see several times later in the play. To drive the point home, Sheridan plays upon Sir Peter's lack of perception. Sir Peter declares confidently, 'I was never mistaken in my life' (line 51), yet he has only a few lines earlier condemned himself by showing his ignorance of the contribution he makes to his quarrels with his wife. Here, at the end of the first act, Sheridan reveals the device of Sir Oliver, the brothers' benefactor, arriving early in order to test the true merit of his nephews, thereby hinting at the disguises, deceptions and revelations that are to come.

CONTEXT

The title **'Man of Sentiment'** (lines 52–3) indicates that Sir Peter approves of Joseph's expressions of moral feelings. Sir Peter uses the term here without the irony of Lady Sneerwell's description of him as **'a sentimental knave'** in Scene 1, line 73.

QUESTION

How do you respond to Sir Peter's character on his first appearance?

GLOSSARY

4	**tiffed** quarrelled
6	**gall** bitterness
13	**plat** plot of ground (an obsolete spelling)
13	**Grosvenor Square** a fashionable district of London
14	**paragraphed** mentioned in newspaper gossip
45	**spark** a high-spirited, fashionable young man
46	**benevolent** generous, charitable
49	**eastern liberality** Sir Oliver's generosity with the riches he has earned in the East Indies (see I.1.315)
74	**consumption** failing health, often caused by tuberculosis
81	**Noll** a shortened form of Oliver

CONTEXT

In an eighteenth century production of the play, Act I Scene 2 and Act II Scene 1, with only two characters in each, would be played close to the audience, with the flats at the side of the stage pulled across to hide Lady Sneerwell's house.

Act II

Scene 1

- Sir Peter and Lady Teazle quarrel over her extravagance.
- She leaves for Lady Sneerwell's, where he will follow her.

This scene takes place a little later in Sir Peter Teazle's house. Sir Peter and Lady Teazle are seen quarrelling; she asserts her right to her 'own way in everything' (line 3), he objects to her extravagance. He reminds her of her humble country background, she insists she needs to be in fashion now she is his wife. When she informs him she is going to Lady Sneerwell's, he criticises the attacks the scandal school makes on people's reputations, but she protests she bears no ill will to those she slanders. As she leaves she reminds him that he promised to join her there.

COMMENTARY

Sheridan achieves another contrast in this scene. Following the friendly conversation of the two older men in Act I Scene 2, we have visible and audible evidence of Sir Peter's 'punishment' for marrying a young wife (I.1.87).

His fury is evident in the first line – as is his powerlessness in the face of his wife's fiery spirit. Lady Teazle's first words on stage repeat the terminology of her husband's outburst to make plain that she will have the better of him in every argument. Her assertion, 'I ought to have my own way in everything' (lines 2–3), is in direct defiance of the expected social order. In response to each attempt by Sir Peter to assert his authority she has a quick answer. She reminds him he is old enough to be her father (lines 10–11) and she only married him to escape from the dullness of country life (lines 29–30). She even goes so far as to imply that she looks forward to being his widow (lines 59–60). There is, however, a hint in Lady Teazle's reference to 'our daily jangle' in line 80 that their arguing is more a kind of game than a threat to their marriage. This is confirmed in Sir Peter's words to the audience after she has left; he clearly still loves her and 'there is great satisfaction in quarrelling with her' (lines 105–6).

The scene is a superb display of verbal sparring and wit, delighting the audience by giving full rein to the skills of the accomplished actors Sheridan had at his disposal at Drury Lane. In many ways this is a classic husband and wife comic routine, with Lady Teazle sweetly turning each objection of her husband to her advantage. Sheridan presents Sir Peter as authoritarian and penny-pinching –

CONTEXT

Frances Abington (1737–1815), who played Lady Teazle, was a leader of fashion. When Sheridan took over Drury Lane in 1776 she negotiated a doubling of her costume allowance to £120. 'No one, it was said, could handle a fan more delightfully or point a witty phrase more gracefully' (Kelly, *Richard Brinsley Sheridan: A Life*, p. 78).

? QUESTION

Compare Lady Teazle's description of her **'disagreeable'** country existence (line 29) with the picture she paints in the Epilogue of her imagined future with her husband back in the country, 'in a lone rustic hall forever pounded' (Epilogue, line 23).

QUESTION

Do you sympathise more with Sir Peter or Lady Teazle in this scene? Can you explain why?

and increasingly angry, often resorting to oaths or exaggeration ('a pair of white cats' to draw her coach, for example, line 50) as a sign of his fury. When he objects to the money she spent on flowers in winter, with artful naivety she blames the weather for the cost, not her extravagance. Their argument reaches a neat conclusion when Lady Teazle smartly turns the lack of taste she showed when she married Sir Peter against him (lines 76–9). What can seem lifeless on the page comes to life when given voice by skilled actors.

The scene does little to advance the plot other than give Sir Peter a reason to call at Lady Sneerwell's – supposedly to defend his reputation. This allows Sheridan to remind us of the scandal school and the damage that, in Sir Peter's eyes at least, they cause.

GLOSSARY

8	**'Slife** an oath: 'God's life'
20	**Pantheon** large public building in Oxford Street, London, used for concerts and entertainments
20	*fête champêtre* picnic party
26	**Oons** another oath: 'God's wounds' (also in another form, 'Zounds', in line 76)
33	**tambour** embroidery frame
39	**receipt-book** recipe book
44	**Pope Joan** card game
49	*vis-à-vis* carriage where the two passengers sit opposite each other
50	**chair** sedan chair, a closed seat carried by footmen
88	**rid on a hurdle** been dragged to execution on a wooden sledge
88–9	**utterers, coiners, clippers** a reference to the similarity between scandalmongers and forgers (those who 'utter' false currency) and currency cheats, who would clip the edges of coins to make new ones

SCENE 2

- Lady Sneerwell is entertaining the scandal school to tea and cards.
- The group mock the appearance and behaviour of a number of their acquaintances.
- Sir Peter arrives, makes his displeasure clear, then leaves.
- When Joseph and Maria are left alone he professes his loves for her, kneeling to do so.
- At this point Lady Teazle enters and Joseph struggles to disguise his romantic overture to Maria, in order to convince Lady Teazle that he loves only her.

The scene moves back to Lady Sneerwell's house, where the scandal school is assembling to take tea, play cards and gossip. Sir Benjamin recites a typically foolish verse he has composed. Lady Sneerwell ensures that Maria sits with Joseph to play cards. After several reputations have been demolished, Sir Peter enters 'to spoil our pleasantry', as his wife says (line 73). Sir Peter's **asides** provide a critical commentary on the continuing character assassinations, until he makes his displeasure known to the company. He leaves and all the others except Maria and Joseph move to another room for cards. Joseph attempts to win some sign of affection from Maria; when she does not respond he goes down on his knees to her. At this point Lady Teazle enters from the rear of the stage and catches Joseph by surprise, so that he has to invent a story to cover his real intentions. He is keen to persuade Lady Teazle that he was attempting to keep his feelings for her from Sir Peter by allaying Maria's suspicions. Although Lady Teazle seems convinced she appears to be keeping him at arm's length. Joseph is left at the end of scene to lament the problem he has caused himself.

CONTEXT

An early **prompt book** describes the set: "'Pembroke table on, and tea things ... Servant attending the company with tea; card table, six striped chairs before the scene'". The 'scene' was the painted scenery flat at the back of the stage, with a central door through which the actors would leave when they move to the next room at line 183.

COMMENTARY

Sheridan uses the first part of the scene to provide further amusing examples of the malicious delight the 'crew' (II.1.88) take in criticising members of their own circle and even, in Mrs Candour's

QUESTION

How does Lady Teazle behave in the company of the scandal school? Has she learnt to be as malicious as the others or does she merely take her cues from them?

CONTEXT

'Miss Pope, "the perfect gentlewoman" was said to be type-cast as Mrs Candour [after taking this role in the original production]; off stage as well as on, her sweetness had a hidden sting' (Kelly, *Richard Brinsley Sheridan: A Life*, p. 78).

case, her own relations. The tone is mostly comic, with Lady Sneerwell's set providing many cruel jokes at the expense of their acquaintances in society – only Maria and Sir Peter show disapproval, though the moral stance of these two is important. The plot develops only a little: we learn that Lady Teazle believes Joseph to be in love with her and is willing to give him some limited encouragement, preparing the way for their clandestine meeting later. This causes him to be caught out when he is seeking to woo Maria. His final words, 'I doubt I shall be exposed at last' (lines 245–6), point to the ending of the play.

Lady Teazle demonstrates that she has acquired some of the scandal school's skill in making cruel comments. The greater part of the gossip, however, is led by Mrs Candour, who provides a steady supply of names for the rest of the gang, despite her protests that 'I never will join in ridiculing a friend' (line 117). Sheridan, of course, makes sure that she criticises someone in every speech. His dialogue for her is particularly skilful; see how he turns her 'defence' of Miss Sallow, 'a near relation', into cruelty with her comment that 'a woman labours under many disadvantages who tries to pass for a girl at six and thirty' (lines 95–9). She keeps up the attack in her next speech, when she makes sure the company is told about her relation's lack of education and poor family (103–6). Her breathless sentences give the impression that she cannot wait to tell us more of each person's faults: listen to the way she delivers additional humiliating revelations about Miss Sallow with 'for let me tell you ...', 'and then as to ...' and 'for you know ...' in lines 97, 103 and 105. An actor playing Mrs Candour requires considerable skill in pacing to negotiate her long and apparently shapeless comments.

Crabtree and Sir Benjamin confirm the impression given in Act I that they are affected fops full of their own importance. Sir Benjamin's poem, like his character, lacks any substance. Sir Peter maintains his hostility, which is clear in the bluntness of his aside: 'A character dead at every word' (line 75). Joseph says little in the first part of the scene, keeping his distance from the scandalmongering; his comment to Sir Benjamin in line 17 may be approving but could be a sarcastic indication that he realises how ridiculous the poem is. His words when he is alone with Maria appear to share her disapproval – but is he right to say of the group that 'they have no malice at heart' (lines 190–1)? Here again Sheridan shows his skill with dialogue; in Joseph's short speech on p. 77 (lines 195–9), his artfully constructed 'sentiments' (quite unlike the thoughtless tumble of Mrs Candour's speech) appear to condemn slander whilst allowing that a speaker may 'falsify from revenge' (line 197). Maria sees through him; her words lack wit but she conveys clearly her disapproval of Joseph's disloyalty to his brother (see lines 206–7). Lady Teazle is more sophisticated: she realises Joseph is playing some kind of game (though unlike the audience she does not know that his real interest is Maria and not herself). However, her response to him is ambiguous; she declares she will not be unfaithful to her husband but tells Joseph, 'I admit you as a lover', even if only as far as 'fashion requires' (line 228).

? QUESTION

Sir Peter says to Lady Sneerwell: 'true wit is more nearly allied to good nature than your ladyship is aware of' (lines 147–8). How do you think an audience would react to the 'wit' displayed in this scene – enjoy it or condemn it, or even both?

GLOSSARY

6	**Curricle** a type of light, two-wheeled carriage, drawn by two horses
7–8	**duodecimo phaeton** another type of small horse-drawn carriage
12	**macaronis** fops (extravagantly dressed men, dandies)
17	**Phoebus** Phoebus (also called Phoebus Apollo) was the Greek god of poetry
23	**piquet** card game for two players
53	**Ochre** a kind of yellow-brown earth used in painting
53	**caulks** fills the cracks
80	**Pursy** fat and short of breath
81	**Codille** a term from the eighteenth-century card game ombre
88	**the Ring** riding area in Hyde Park, London
106	**sugar-baker** maker of loaf sugar, a refined form of sugar compacted into a loaf shape
113	**Stucco** plaster, used to cover cracks in walls
115	**French fruit** hollow sweets containing mottoes
128	**teeth *à la Chinoise*** black, as if from eating opium. Opium was imported from China at this time

continued

SCENE 2 continued

CONTEXT

This scene makes use of the full depth of the Drury Lane stage. Sir Peter comes to the forestage, in front of the **proscenium arch**, to make his **asides**. The distance to the rear of the stage gave opportunity for the actors to leave, in the words of one early manuscript stage direction, 'all talking as they are going to the next room' and it also enables Lady Teazle to enter unobserved by Maria and Joseph, who are downstage near the audience.

129	***table d'hôte* at Spa** dining table at an inn in the Belgian town of Spa, famous for its mineral water springs. Visiting spas was a fashionable craze for the upper classes in the 1700s
156	**manors** landed estates
157	**Act for the Preservation of Fame** Sir Peter's response sounds like a real Act for the Preservation of Game (that is, game birds shot for sport) and is one of his few attempts at wit
166	**law merchant** that is, a law about trading in gossip; this image continues with 'slander currency' (line 167), that is, circulating slander like money, where a 'drawer' writes the cheque and the 'endorser' signs it (line 169)
229	**Platonic *cicisbeo*** an admirer of a married woman (but not her lover – the relationship is 'Platonic', that is, not involving a sexual relationship)
240	**politics** schemes

SCENE 3

- Rowley informs Sir Oliver of Sir Peter's marriage and of the contrasting reputations of Charles and Joseph.
- Sir Peter tells Sir Oliver of his high regard for Joseph, while Charles is 'a lost young man'.
- Sir Oliver refuses to take these reputations at face value and announces his intention to put the brothers to the test.

The action returns to Sir Peter's house (an 'Antique Chamber' in the words of one contemporary **prompt book**). Rowley is talking to Sir Oliver, Joseph and Charles Surface's uncle, who has returned to England after making his fortune in India. Sir Oliver is amused to learn that his old friend is married, though he is warned by Rowley not to mock Sir Peter for it – Rowley needs to repeat this warning later in the scene. Sir Oliver is informed that Joseph is Sir Peter's favourite, but he is dismissive of any evidence based on reputation alone, and promises to rescue Charles if he 'has done nothing false or mean' (line 21). After a little banter with Sir Peter about his 'happy state' of matrimony (line 44), the talk turns back to the Surface brothers, whom Sir Peter has looked after while their uncle was abroad. Although Sir Peter speaks highly of Joseph's 'noblest sentiments' (lines 60–1), confirming his prejudice against Charles, Sir Oliver is sceptical; he will put their characters to the test.

COMMENTARY

Sheridan varies the pace again by following the brilliant public display of wit at Lady Sneerwell's with a short, intimate scene and a quite different kind of morality. Sir Oliver's good humour at his old friend's expense is a much gentler type of mockery than that seen in the previous scene, and he is forthright in his condemnation of the 'malicious, prating, prudent gossips ... who murder characters to kill time' (lines 16–18). Sir Oliver will apply different standards from the scandal school (and by implication, polite society in general) when judging the Surface brothers. As we have already seen Joseph behave in ways that are 'false or mean' (line 21), it seems clear which brother their uncle will prefer.

From the point of view of the plot, this scene merely introduces Sir Oliver and announces that he and Rowley have planned a test of the brothers' characters. More importantly, however, it establishes the character of Sir Oliver as someone who, supported by Rowley, stands for a simpler, more generous standard of morality. He is willing to forgive Charles' extravagance, recalling that he and his brother (the father of Joseph and Charles) were also reckless in their youth, and his response to Sir Peter's praise of Joseph's 'sentiments' (line 61) makes it clear that, unlike his friend, he is not going to be deceived by fine words: 'Oh, plague of his sentiments! If he salutes me with a scrap of morality in his mouth, I shall be sick directly' (lines 62–3). In contrast to what he considers the false and superficial 'sentiments' of Joseph, Sir Oliver intends to expose what is in 'their hearts' (line 66), where, it is implied, he hopes genuine emotion is to be found.

? QUESTION

Sir Peter and Sir Oliver are similar in age and good friends, but what contrasts does Sheridan create between the two here? How are these contrasts developed in the next scene?

GLOSSARY

2	**stood bluff** stuck firmly (to his bachelor state)
7	**stool of repentance** in Scottish churches, the stool where sinners sat during services
16	**prudent** here this means calculating or worldly wise (and again at line 75)
21	**compound** settle up (that is, clear his debts)
53	**character** reputation in society
72	***Allons*** let's go
74	**Odds my life!** an oath: 'God's my life!'

ACT III

SCENE 1

- Rowley explains to Sir Peter and Sir Oliver his plan to test the brothers by using the character of a poor relation called Mr Stanley.
- Sir Peter devises a different plan for Sir Oliver to pretend to be a moneylender.
- Sir Peter seeks to persuade Maria to marry Joseph but she refuses. He dismisses her in a fury.
- Lady Teazle charms Sir Peter into giving her money.
- They are soon arguing again, however, and he threatens to divorce her, accusing her of being in love with Charles.

This scene takes place in the same room in Sir Peter's house, though the fresh act indicates the passage of a short period of time, during which we are to assume Rowley has begun to explain in detail his plan to test the Surface brothers. Sir Oliver is to pretend to be a poor relation from Dublin, Mr Stanley, who asks each of the brothers for help – Sir Oliver can then observe their responses. Rowley has also invited Moses, a moneylender, to explain Charles'

CONTEXT

The line, 'a merchant in Dublin' (line 5), is perhaps a private reference to Sheridan's own family history; his father had to leave Dublin to escape his creditors. After the play was written, when he was a Member of Parliament, Sheridan was often asked to help his Irish relatives to government positions.

financial affairs. Whilst talking to Moses, Sir Peter hits on the idea that Sir Oliver should accompany Moses as a Mr Premium in order to observe Charles at first hand. Sir Oliver is delighted with this scheme and takes pleasure in learning how to talk like a moneylender.

Sir Peter's interview with Maria is unhappy. She has agreed not to see Charles but will not obey Sir Peter and marry Joseph. As she leaves, Lady Teazle enters and succeeds in charming her husband into giving her £200. For a while they appear happily reconciled as they recall when they first met. However, when Sir Peter asserts that his wife always begins any argument they are soon quarrelling so bitterly that he accuses her of having an affair with Charles and ends by promising a separate maintenance for her or even a divorce. Lady Teazle happily agrees, leaving her husband furious that he can't even make her angry.

CONTEXT

It seems that Stanley has been imprisoned for debt, as was the practice at the time, but is now allowed temporary release to try to raise money (see lines 15–16). Many years later Sheridan himself spent some time in sponging-houses (debtors' prisons).

COMMENTARY

The high point of this scene – and one of the highlights of the play – is the tempestuous quarrel between Sir Peter and Lady Teazle that brings it to a dramatic conclusion. First, however, Sheridan explains the rather cumbersome plot to test the brothers, introducing yet more deception – though in this case in the interests of discovering the truth rather than disguising villainy. Apart from establishing that Maria will refuse, at whatever cost, to marry Joseph and thus confirming her position as a helpless victim, the main point of this section of the scene is to develop Sheridan's portrayal of his characters. Rowley continues to defend Charles to Sir Peter, reporting that despite his financial problems Charles has done what he can to help Stanley – quoting Shakespeare on Prince Hal's generous spirit (lines 22–3). Unlike Sir Peter, Rowley is portrayed as seeing beyond the surface and discerning the true qualities of the younger brother. Sir Oliver shares Rowley's good judgement and is obviously sympathetic to Charles ('Ah, he is my brother's son', line 13). Thus, the audience is made aware of the possibility of rescue for the young lovers, particularly as Rowley mentions that he will call upon Snake to give evidence too.

CONTEXT

King Henry's words on Prince Hal are taken from Shakespeare's *Henry IV Part 2*, IV.4.31–2. Prince Hal, having apparently wasted his youth in bad company, reforms dramatically and ultimately becomes the victor of Agincourt in *Henry V*. Charles, it is implied, will also reveal his noble qualities by the end of this play.

> **CONTEXT**
>
> Robert Baddeley, the actor who took the part of Moses in 1777, specialised in foreigners; the text includes an example of ungrammatical English in 'want the moneys very bad' (lines 94–5) and Baddeley may have introduced others.

Sir Oliver clearly enjoys the opportunity of accompanying Moses in the guise of a broker to learn some of the tricks of the moneylender's trade – in the process, Sheridan touches on contemporary concerns about high rates of interest and the exploitation of borrowers. Sheridan's portrayal of Moses, the 'friendly Jew' (line 29) is a relatively sympathetic one though a modern audience might find some of the assumptions close to anti-Semitic. Sheridan does make it clear that the real Mr Premium, who plans to lend money to Charles, is a Christian, though Sir Oliver's comment that he is 'very sorry to hear it' (line 77) implies that Moses' profession is an unsavoury one, and is unsuitable for Christians.

Sir Peter confirms his obstinacy with his words and behaviour in each part of this scene. He refuses to think well of Charles when told of his desire to help Stanley, his behaviour to Maria is domineering and his temper gets the better of him in the dispute with Lady Teazle, allowing her a complete victory. Yet it is again clear that he loves her: 'How happy I should be if I could tease her into loving me, though but a little' (lines 166–7). As a result she is easily able to obtain money from him in return for little more than giving him her hand to kiss (line 179). Sheridan's dialogue for both of the Teazles is magnificent in this scene. Lady Teazle's control over her husband is complete – his loss of temper is a triumph and she leaves him with a laugh, having won not only the £200 but also the promise of a separate income (line 249). Sheridan ensures that she has the first word as well as the last, teasing him for quarrelling with someone other than herself as soon as she enters (lines 168–9). Once she has the money, she is content to humour him – but only on her terms: 'I'm sure I don't care how soon we leave off quarrelling provided you'll own you were tired first' (lines 183–4). Even when talking pleasantly of their courtship she introduces subtle reminders of his age (see lines 196–8).

> **CONTEXT**
>
> The £200 Lady Teazle asks for in line 174 is a substantial sum: we learn in Act III Scene 2 that the servant Trip earns £50 a year (line 25).

Sheridan turns the apparent reconciliation into an escalating row when Sir Peter, obstinate as ever, tries to blame his wife for their quarrels. As the pace increases, their endearments ('my dear Sir Peter', 'my angel!', 'my love', 'my dear', lines 208–17) are spoken with increasingly savage **irony** until Lady Teazle furiously accuses him of being 'a great bear' (line 226) and makes a hurtful comment about 'an old dangling bachelor, who was single at fifty only because he never could meet with anyone who would have him' (lines 234–6). Her reference to a suitor she refused is barbed – Sir Tivy Terrier would have been a better choice because he is now dead and she would have his estate (lines 239–41). When Sir Peter mentions the rumours linking Lady Teazle and Charles, she warns him 'I'll not be suspected without cause' (line 248), raising the possibility that she might indeed betray him (though we know that her interest is in Joseph). Sir Peter is left on stage, defeated, at the end, revealing that he still feels for her but cannot bear to see her have the upper hand all the time.

CONTEXT

Sheridan carefully rehearsed the climax of this scene (lines 224–55) with Mrs Abington. 'That will not do,' he said. 'It must not be pettish. That's shallow, shallow! You must go up the stage with, "You are just like my cousin Sophy said you would be", and then turn and sweep down on Sir Peter like a volcano' (cited in Kelly, *Richard Brinsley Sheridan: A Life*, p. 80).

GLOSSARY

2	**jet** point, purpose
39	**evidence** witness
60	**Crutched Friars** a street in the City of London
65	**romancing** fantastic, unbelievable
76	**principal** a legal term – here, it means the chief lender
82	**cant** jargon
83	**treating** bargaining
109	**run out** complain about
110	**Annuity Bill** this Bill, being debated in Parliament when the play was first performed, would curb the power of moneylenders; interest would be limited and contracts with minors (those under the age of twenty-one) were to be outlawed. It became law later in 1777
165	**helpmate** an ironic reference to the creation of Eve to be 'an help meet' for Adam in the Book of Genesis (2:18)
239	**Tivy Terrier** a name derived from hunting terms ('tantivy' is a hunting cry, especially one made at full gallop)

SCENE 2

- Moses and Sir Oliver (disguised as Mr Premium) arrive at Charles' house where they are met by the servant, Trip.
- Trip takes the opportunity to seek a loan of £20 from Moses.

In a room in Charles' house, Moses and Sir Oliver (pretending to be Mr Premium) are met by the servant Trip. The servant has learnt some extravagance from his master and asks Moses if he can borrow £20, with some of Charles' clothes as a guarantee.

COMMENTARY

After the storm of the previous scene, Sheridan allows a short moment of calm before the audience is taken into the noisy party at Charles' house. The scene adds little to the plot but provides a brilliant cameo role for Philip La Mash, who first played Trip. The servant's behaviour confirms that recklessness with money has spread throughout the household, and he displays an amusing array of social pretensions. He leaves after five lines, taking snuff like a gentleman, and on his return reveals that he has adopted the fashionable affectations of wearing an ornament in his hair and buying bouquets of flowers. It is therefore no surprise that he is short of money – and in any case Charles is often in arrears with the wages. He has learnt to borrow as well as to dress like a gentleman, using Charles' cast-off clothes as surety; he has already asked Moses for a loan on a previous visit, though his credit is not good enough. Sir Oliver is shocked by the extravagance, but Sheridan also takes the opportunity to demonstrate once more that he values emotion over calculation: Joseph is condemned in lines 11–12 because although (as elder son) he inherited the family home he was more interested in the money and sold it to his brother.

CONTEXT

A manuscript **prompt book** indicates that a backcloth would be let down on a roller to show that this scene takes place in an antechamber in Charles' house. This would be raised at the beginning of the next scene to reveal Charles and his friends drinking round a table.

GLOSSARY

21	place position, job
26	bag a silk or satin bag tied to the hair with a decorative bow was a feature of fashionable men's dress at the time

27	**bastinadoes** beatings, usually on the soles of the feet. Sir Oliver's violent exclamation indicates his contempt for Trip's attempts to copy the latest fashions
29	**bill discounted** (a discounted bill) a note promising money, with commission deducted when it is cashed
38	**annuity** loan with annual interest payable on it (see Act III Scene 1 for information on the Annuity Bill)
46–51	**capital … security** these financial terms show Trip has learnt the language of moneylending from his master; 'equity of redemption', for example, means the right to be repaid a loan
49	**reversion … obit** a reversion indicates money to be paid on someone's death (here it will be paid when Charles passes on his coat for Trip to sell); a *post obit* is similarly secured on expectation of being repaid when the borrower inherits money after the death of another
51	**point ruffles** frills made from a kind of lace called point lace, worn at the wrist

QUESTION

Trip's character and his request for a loan add nothing important to the plot – so why do you think Sheridan included this scene?

SCENE 3

- Charles and his friends are drinking; he proposes a toast to Maria and they sing in praise of women.
- Moses and Sir Oliver arrive and Charles attempts to negotiate a loan; as almost everything of value has been sold Charles has little to offer as security.
- Sir Oliver eventually agrees to buy the family portraits from Charles, who still does not realise that 'Mr Premium' is his uncle in disguise.

QUESTION

This is the first appearance of Charles. How does Sheridan create a contrast with his older brother here?

A party is in progress in Charles' house. Charles and his friends talk in praise of drinking, and when the conversation turns to women he proposes a toast to Maria. Sir Harry, in reply, sings a song in praise of all women. Trip announces Moses and Mr Premium (that is, Sir Oliver) and Charles proposes a toast to usury, or money lending. Sir Oliver, less keen on debt, attempts to change the toast and in response Careless and the others try to make him drink a pint

SCENE 3 continued

bumper, in other words, a pint glass filled to the brim. Charles intervenes and ushers his friends into the next room whilst he negotiates his loan. Sir Oliver pretends that he has to raise the money from a friend and asks Charles what security he can offer. Charles, having little else, offers a promise to pay on the death of his rich uncle – who, as the audience realise but he does not, is standing in front of him. Sir Oliver then asks what there is to sell, only to learn that the silver and library have, to his horror, already been disposed of. Charles offers to auction his family portraits and Sir Oliver agrees to buy them although he is furious at what he considers an insult to their ancestors.

CONTEXT

Sir Harry's song, with music by Thomas Linley, Sheridan's father-in-law, was an immediate hit with audiences. Soon the playbills for *The School for Scandal* were announcing the song as a special feature: 'In Act III a song by Mr Vernon'. Joseph Vernon (1738–82) was a celebrated Drury Lane singer who played Sir Harry in 1780.

COMMENTARY

The scene shows Charles, on his first appearance, in a jovial mood. For Sir Oliver, the scene confirms what he has heard about the younger son's extravagance but (worse for Charles) his uncle is horrified at the way the young man has disposed of the family's assets. Charles is respectful towards Moses and 'Mr Premium' but the audience learn that Sir Oliver is so horrified at the sale of the family portraits that he'll 'never forgive him this – never' (line 223). It seems that Charles' fate, which had looked brighter at the arrival of the originally sympathetic Sir Oliver, will take a turn for the worst after all.

WWW. CHECK THE NET

Joseph Vernon is listed as one of the regular performers at Vauxhall Gardens, a hugely popular outdoor entertainment venue in eighteenth-century London. Go to **www.vauxhallgardens.com** to find out more. Joseph Vernon can be found under the list of 'Singers'.

The plot is developing towards a crisis. Earlier scenes have hinted that Joseph may be about to be exposed as a fraud (see Rowley's allusion in Act III Scene 1 to catching Snake in 'a matter little short of forgery', lines 40–1), but now Charles is in danger of losing the one friend who can rescue him – and his relationship with Maria. For the audience, this rise in tension is accomplished in a lively scene, a contrast to both the discussion in the antechamber and the Teazles' domestic argument. After Charles and the aptly-named Careless praise the virtues of drink, we are reminded of Charles' real love for Maria, before Sir Harry's rousing song has them all joining the chorus. Although supposedly in praise of 'superlative' beauty (line 35), the song is much more down-to-earth: they drink to all women, 'bashful fifteen' or 'widow of fifty' (lines 40–1), taking delight in them all – a contrast to the cruel criticism of older women made by the scandal school.

The scheme to encourage Charles to reveal his true nature to the disguised Sir Oliver works well. Although he praises drink before Moses and his uncle arrive, and has them join in a toast to usury, he prevents Careless from forcing 'Mr Premium' to pay a penalty for altering the toast. When they are alone, he comes straight to the point: he knows that his ungoverned spending has got himself into a state where he will have to pay an exorbitant rate of interest. His references to Sir Oliver are a source of humour; as he talks of the old man's impending death the audience wonder if Sir Oliver will give himself away – or if Charles will say something so outrageous that he loses his uncle's favour. Sheridan makes the device of the disguise explicit when Charles says his uncle is 'so much altered lately, that his nearest relations don't know him' (lines 173–4), and the audience joins in Sir Oliver's laughter at Charles' unconscious **irony** – he has, indeed, not recognised the old man. Sir Oliver is also outspoken – though only by means of **asides**. His increasing anger contrasts with Charles' cheerful account of the disposal of his fortune to give the impression that Charles' hopes of inheritance may be fading.

? QUESTION

How well does Sir Oliver play the part of Mr Premium? How does Sheridan exploit the fact that the 'little broker' is actually Charles' uncle?

GLOSSARY

12	**play** here, this means playing cards or gambling
14	**hazard** a gambling game played with two dice
23	**bumpers** brimming glasses
29	**canonized vestals** virgin saints; vestal comes from the Roman goddess Vesta whose sacred fire was tended by virgin priestesses
42	**quean** a boisterous, impudent woman
75	**conscientious** that is, their consciences will trouble them (about charging exorbitant rates)
83	**sentiment** a toast – an alternative meaning for a word much used in the play, usually to mean moral feelings
89	**demurred** challenged the toast (by changing the wording)
139	**beau-pot** bough-pot – a decorative pot with holes in for holding cut branches
172	**breaks apace** his health is quickly deteriorating
216–17	**no bowels for** no affection or feeling for

continued

SCENE 3 continued

218 **Shylock** In Shakespeare's *The Merchant of Venice* (c. 1596), Antonio borrows money from Shylock, promising to forfeit a pound of his own flesh if he fails to repay it

ACT IV

SCENE 1

- Careless begins the auction of Charles' family portraits.
- They start with individual portraits but Charles soon becomes impatient and offers to sell the rest of the collection for £300.
- He refuses, however, to sell the portrait of Sir Oliver even when offered double the total sum.
- Sir Oliver forgives Charles 'everything' for this sign of affection and writes him a cheque for twice the total anyway.
- Charles asks Rowley to cash the cheque and give £100 to Stanley, despite Rowley's protests that he should use the money for his own bills.

The curtain rises on a picture gallery and we are to assume the characters have arrived straight from the previous scene. Careless uses an old parchment of the family tree as both a hammer and a catalogue for the collection. After settling on prices for about ten pictures, Charles tires of the auction and offers to sell the rest for £300, to which Sir Oliver agrees. He has noticed that Charles has passed over one picture – the one of himself, painted before he went to India. Despite Careless' tactless description of the sitter as 'an inveterate knave' (line 92), Charles refuses to part with the picture – even when offered as much for it as Sir Oliver is paying for the rest of the collection – because 'Noll' has been good to him. This wins Sir Oliver's affection and he writes Charles a cheque for double the amount nonetheless, saying he'll send for the pictures later.

CHECK THE BOOK

The original set for this scene would have had the Surface family portraits painted onto the back flat. The scenery was designed by Philip James de Loutherbourg (1740–1812), a painter from Alsace who had been appointed by Garrick to Drury Lane. His dramatic designs were much admired for their realism. You can read an account of eighteenth-century theatres in the relevant chapter of Phyllis Hartnoll's *The Theatre: A Concise History* (Thames and Hudson, 1998), which contains helpful illustrations including an engraving of the 'screen scene' (Act IV Scene 3).

When Rowley arrives, Charles asks him to cash the cheque and take £100 immediately to his poor relation Stanley. Rowley protests that he should be wiser with his money but Charles will not be deterred from his generosity.

COMMENTARY

By the end of this scene, the audience knows that Charles' fortunes have turned, even though he himself does not yet realise it. He has proved his good nature to Sir Oliver by his affection for his portrait, and in addition his generosity to Mr Stanley will, we know, soon be reported to Sir Oliver by Rowley (in fact this happens before they leave Charles' house, in the next scene). This is an important plot development as we approach the play's climax at the end of this Act. The rowdiness with Charles' friends in the last scene gives way to an episode which, whilst comic in its own way, is more concerned with generosity, loyalty and affection – genuine sentiments, in other words, in contrast to Joseph's empty words.

The portrayal of Charles' character is at least as important – for it is his good nature that convinces Sir Oliver that his nephew is 'an honest fellow' by line 116, despite swearing 'I'll never forgive him' in the previous scene (III.3.223). Charles maintains his good humour and high spirits throughout the scene – and indeed at all other times. As Rowley says, 'There's no making you serious a moment' (line 155). This is likely to make him attractive to the audience as well as to his uncle: unlike his brother, Charles says what he feels and appears incapable of deception. Unlike the scandal school, he seems unconcerned about appearances and affectations; he's happy to sell off the pictures of all his famous relations, accompanying the sale with humorous descriptions of the sitters. When Sir Oliver has left, his good nature is proved in a practical way when he sends part of the money he has been given to his poor relation, even though it means not paying some of his own debts. This impulsive, kind-hearted action is also likely to endear him to the audience – the play encourages little sympathy for the tradesmen Charles is indebted to, who are described by Careless as 'the most exorbitant fellows' (line 136).

CONTEXT

'Modern Raphael' (line 6) would have been understood by the audience as a reference to Sir Joshua Reynolds (1723–92), famous for his idealised portraits. He was a friend of the Sheridans and had already painted them both, including 'Mrs Sheridan as St Cecilia' (the patron saint of music), which Reynolds considered the finest picture he had ever painted.

CONTEXT

By cruel **irony**, when Sheridan was deep in debt in the last year of his life he had to sell many of his own pictures, including Reynolds' portrait of Elizabeth as St Cecilia. The Sheridan family already had experience of selling up to pay off creditors; when Richard was eight the family's possessions were put up for auction in Ireland and this may have provided ideas for this scene.

Sir Oliver also stays true to character here, speaking his feelings freely to the audience. These **asides** form a running commentary on the family members in the portraits (Sir Oliver of course knows their histories), providing a comic counterpoint to Charles' own descriptions. By the end of the scene, he's even praising Charles to his face. Like Charles, Sir Oliver is impulsive in his responses, moving from angry condemnation of his nephew in the previous scene to enthusiastic endorsement by the end of this one. His generosity seems to be as extravagant as Charles' spending – when he says of Charles, 'how like his father the dog is!' (line 109), the audience may recall Sir Oliver's earlier revelation that he and his brother were similarly rash (II.3.27).

See **Extended commentaries – Text 2** for further discussion of this scene.

GLOSSARY

2	**up to the Conquest** back as far as the Norman Conquest of England in 1066
5	**no volunteer … expression** no voluntary gracefulness has been given them by the painter
15	**gouty chair** chair with a leg rest for those suffering from gout, an inflammation of the foot
23	***ex post facto* parricide** killing one's parents (parricide) after the event (by 'knocking them down') – Charles means the auctioneer's hammer knocks when the price is agreed (line 22), but Sir Oliver plays on the literal meaning – that Charles is killing them off
24	**generation** genealogy, family tree
29	**Raveline** a ravelin is a form of embankment fortification, so is an appropriate name for a general
31	**Malplaquet** battle in War of the Spanish Succession (1701–14) between the French and, chiefly, England and the Dutch Republic, which took place in 1709
41	**Kneller** Sir Godfrey Kneller, a famous portrait painter (1676–1723), patronised by William III and George IV
44	**five pounds ten** five pounds ten shillings
49	**beaux** young men of fashion; in Sheridan's time, men wore their hair powdered and the women wore tall wigs

60	**the woolsack** the woolsack was the official seat of the Lord Chancellor in the House of Lords (the seat itself was stuffed with wool), but here it stands for judges in general
125	**nabob** rich East India Company official
130	**genius** nature
150	**splenetic** bad tempered
166	**beldame** an old woman, especially an ugly or malicious one

SCENE 2

- Sir Oliver and Moses are on their way out of Charles' house when Rowley brings Sir Oliver the gift from Charles to Stanley.
- Trip, as he shows them out, takes the opportunity to ask Moses again about a loan.

Back in the antechamber of Charles' house, as in Act III Scene 2, Moses points out that they have now seen how extravagant Charles is but Sir Oliver can think only of his nephew's refusal to part with the portrait of him. Rowley delivers the £100 Charles has sent for Stanley, confirming his good reputation in Sir Oliver's eyes. Sir Oliver promises to pay Charles' outstanding debts and now plans to test Joseph's virtue. The scene ends with Trip again talking to Moses about raising some money.

COMMENTARY

This short scene rounds off Charles' trial by proving him to be generous in deed as well as in family affection. Sir Oliver's repetition that his nephew 'would not sell my picture' in lines 3, 5 and 7 shows he is completely won over by the young man. Perhaps we are also meant to detect some vanity in the ease with which Sir Oliver is influenced – even before he has heard of Charles' generosity to Stanley he has changed his mind about Charles. As Sir Oliver announces that he will now turn his attention to Joseph, Trip

CHECK THE NET

There is a portrait of Robert Baddeley as Moses (a part he played over 200 times) on the website of the Lady Lever Art Gallery: **www.liverpoolmuseums.org.uk** (go to the homepage and type 'Zoffany' into the search box). The artist, Johann Zoffany (1733–1810), shows Moses as well dressed, which presumably suits his profitable occupation, but he also takes a few liberties with the text by showing him with the family tree under his arm and marking down the portraits as they are sold, when these are Careless' tasks. Some of the family portraits can be seen in the background.

takes Moses aside to renew his request for money, allowing Sheridan to poke further fun at the way the servant imitates his master by living beyond his means. The mention of Sir Peter visiting Joseph ahead of Sir Oliver also prepares us for the next scene.

GLOSSARY

6	**deep** deeply – that is, he spends extravagantly at the gambling table
31	**Birthday clothes** best clothes. In Sheridan's time, fashionable new clothes were traditionally bought to celebrate the king's official birthday

QUESTION

What evidence is there in the text that this is not the first time Lady Teazle has visited Joseph alone?

SCENE 3

- Joseph's planned seduction of Lady Teazle is interrupted by the unexpected arrival of Sir Peter, whereupon Lady Teazle hides behind a screen.
- Sir Peter tells Joseph he suspects his wife is having an affair with Charles and also that he intends to settle money on her.
- They are interrupted by Charles, and Sir Peter hides in the closet to eavesdrop, after spying Joseph's 'French milliner' also hiding in the room.
- Charles denies any interest in Lady Teazle, and instead incriminates Joseph; to keep Charles quiet, Joseph tells him that Sir Peter has overhead them, at which point Charles drags Sir Peter into the room.
- When Joseph is called away, Sir Peter tells Charles about the 'milliner' and Charles knocks down the screen to reveal Lady Teazle just as Joseph reappears.
- Lady Teazle brushes aside Joseph's attempts to explain by confessing to Sir Peter that she would have betrayed him, but hearing of his genuine love for her and his generosity she bitterly regrets her actions.

The scene is Joseph's library. Joseph muses on the delicacy of his situation, wishing to enjoy an affair with Lady Teazle without losing his chance to marry Maria. Lady Teazle arrives and the conversation moves from her annoyance with Sir Peter to Joseph's attempt to persuade her that she should betray her husband. Just as he takes her hand, Sir Peter arrives and Lady Teazle, in panic, hides behind a screen at the back of the stage. Sir Peter has come to seek Joseph's advice on his troubles with Lady Teazle; he tells Joseph that he believes his wife is in love with Charles and he fears the mockery he will suffer if this is discovered. Joseph pretends he cannot believe what Sir Peter says whilst subtly implying it is true. Sir Peter describes the financial settlement he intends to make on Lady Teazle so that she will no longer have reason to argue with him. Joseph is worried that this may soften her heart towards her husband and becomes even more alarmed when Sir Peter begins to talk about Joseph's progress in his relationship with Maria, fearing Lady Teazle will hear this. He is saved by the arrival of Charles. Sir Peter decides to take the chance to eavesdrop on the conversation. He almost discovers Lady Teazle behind the screen but is persuaded by Joseph it is a 'French milliner' (line 233) and hides in the closet.

Charles laughs off the accusation that he is attempting to seduce Lady Teazle, saying he always thought that she was interested in Joseph. Alarmed that Charles will say too much, Joseph tells his brother that Sir Peter has been listening all the time and Charles promptly pulls him out of his hiding place. They are interrupted again by the servant and whilst Joseph is out of the room, Sir Peter decides it will be amusing to tell Charles about the existence of the other eavesdropper – the 'French milliner'. Delighted, Charles goes to reveal her and knocks down the screen to uncover Lady Teazle just as Joseph returns. After a few moments of stunned silence, Charles leaves them. Joseph begins an explanation but Lady Teazle silences him by confessing that it was indeed true that she was on the point of betraying her husband. She has been moved by his generosity, overheard whilst she was behind the screen, and leaves in shame, denouncing Joseph.

CONTEXT

In Sheridan's time, the convention that an actor could speak directly to the audience in a **soliloquy** (as is common in Shakespeare's plays) was beginning to be criticised as unrealistic, though Joseph's remarks at the beginning of this scene are more in line with the older tradition, ensuring that the audience is aware of the deception he must practise on Lady Teazle.

CONTEXT

Sir Peter's allowance of £800 a year for Lady Teazle is generous. Although Sheridan's notes reveal that Richard Yates, who played Sir Oliver in the first production, was paid an £800 salary by Drury Lane, he was by far the most highly paid of the company.

COMMENTARY

This, the climax of the play, is also the longest scene. The events follow a complicated pattern of deceptions, as the characters enter, hide and are revealed. The famous 'screen scene', that caused such a sensation on the first night, is all about revelations of one kind or another. Joseph's deceptions are revealed and his sentiments exposed as hypocrisy. Lady Teazle's flirtation is uncovered – and she sees her folly for what it is. Sir Peter is shown to be bigger hearted than his wife believed and she declares her gratitude. Although we cannot at this point be sure they will be reconciled, this looks likely. Charles has proved his innocence to Sir Peter and restored their friendship, especially now that his brother is disgraced. The audience looks forward to the loose ends being tied up in the final act: Joseph has yet to be fully punished and the young lovers will presumably be united.

The tone of this scene, following the rather **sentimental** comedy of Charles' generosity and his uncle's change of heart in Act IV Scene 1, becomes one of pure **farce**. The characters who enter, hide and are revealed do so in quick succession. Joseph, whose villainy was never in doubt, becomes increasingly desperate in his attempts to keep his visitors from discovering each other. At one point Sir Peter and Lady Teazle each peep out of their hiding places in a comic trio with Joseph as he tries to keep them hidden (lines 244–51), only to have Charles, in his usual impetuous way, bring the whole edifice of deception crashing to the floor along with the screen. The audience, witnessing everything that is going on and expecting Joseph to be caught out at any moment, should enjoy this immensely. There is a serious point – Sir Peter's marriage is threatened and Joseph is a heartless hypocrite – but this is less important than the good humour the audience is likely to feel now that Lady Teazle has been saved from total disgrace and Charles has been vindicated in the eyes of Maria's guardian.

The characters mainly conform to the patterns they have established earlier. Joseph's sophisticated sentences are full of deceit, particularly when persuading Lady Teazle that she has a right to 'make a trifling *faux pas*' (in other words, commit adultery, lines

69–70). As he loses control of events, however, his control of language fails too – his speech in lines 382–8 is broken up by numerous dashes to indicate he is for once lost for words. Compare this stuttering performance with his smooth guile earlier in the scene, for example in lines 47–50 where he is justifying to Lady Teazle the very behaviour he cannot later explain to Sir Peter. Lady Teazle almost matches Joseph in the artful construction of her dialogue at the beginning of the scene, though she is too honest to use a word such as '*honour*' when she is about to 'do wrong' (lines 88, 92). She talks of the whole affair as if it is a game, saying of Sir Peter's jealousy of the innocent Charles: 'That's the best of the story, isn't it?' (line 25). When threatened with discovery, however, the truth dawns: 'I'm ruined!' (line 109). By the end she has, in her own words, 'recovered her senses' (line 407) and, in total contrast to Joseph's attempt to justify himself, she confesses her guilt to her husband.

Sheridan's portrayal of Sir Peter is more sympathetic in this scene. Talking to Joseph, whom he feels he can trust, his unhappiness appears more touching than comic, especially when he confesses the additional pain he has been caused by the suspicion that Charles, the nephew of his old friend, has wronged him. In contrast to the tyrannical figure he appeared in his earlier dealings with Lady Teazle and Maria, Sir Peter reveals a magnanimous side to his character, planning a generous settlement for his wife that wins back her affection. His mischievous delight in telling Charles of the 'French milliner' also makes him more human – and more akin to Charles, whose side he now takes rather than that of Joseph. When Lady Teazle is discovered, he doesn't explode with anger, as we might have expected from earlier scenes; his cold comment to Joseph: 'you are a villain!' (line 419) indicates that he has been cured of the young man's 'sentiments'. Charles is here the same good-natured, honest fellow seen in earlier scenes, wasting no time in denying any interest in Lady Teazle but taking the chance to tease his brother about her and so causing Joseph further embarrassment. Sheridan allows Charles to tease the audience too when he says, 'if a pretty woman was purposely to throw herself in my way – and that pretty woman married to a man old enough to be her father – '; the pause and Joseph's interruption of 'Well?' suggest that Charles may

QUESTION

How do you think the actor playing Lady Teazle should behave towards Joseph in their dialogues? Does she take his arguments seriously? Should she appear to be about to give herself to him or act as if merely flattered by his attention? How close Lady Teazle actually is to a 'fall' has important implications for the moral tone of her character.

SCENE 3 continued

CONTEXT

The throwing down of the screen was a triumph on the first night. Twelve-year-old Frederic Reynolds (1764–1841), who was walking down the narrow passage at the side of the theatre about nine o'clock that evening, heard such a terrible noise that, sure the theatre was collapsing, he took to his heels lest he be killed. He 'found the next morning that the noise did not arise from the *falling* of the house, but from the *falling* of the screen in the fourth act; so violent and so tumultuous were the applause and laughter' (cited in O'Toole, *A Traitor's Kiss*, p. 120).

be about to incriminate himself in front of Sir Peter. His conclusion: 'Well, I believe I should be obliged to borrow a little of your morality' (lines 282–7) is both a comic deflation of our expectations and also a satiric comment on Joseph's double standards, since the older brother's 'morality', as we have just seen in his reasoning with Lady Teazle, is highly suspect. As a further sign of his decency, after Charles' impulsive actions have brought Sir Peter and Lady Teazle out into the open, he considerately withdraws rather than take the opportunity for revenge.

See **Extended commentaries – Text 3** for more detailed analysis of Sheridan's theatrical effects in this scene.

GLOSSARY

66	**outrageous** feel outraged
75	**plethora** suffering from an unhealthy fullness
106	***Gaping*** yawning
110	**coxcomb** a foolish fellow – Joseph means he is over-fond of books
199	**sensibly chagrined** extremely disappointed
223	**trepan** entrap
234	**character** here, a good reputation to protect
309	***incog.*** incognito (disguised or hidden)
344	**anchorite** like a hermit, someone who lives a solitary life for religious reasons
351	**be quit with him** get even with him, pay him back
382	**pretensions** claims (as a suitor to Maria)

ACT V

SCENE 1

- Sir Oliver calls on Joseph in the guise of poor Stanley, seeking financial help, having been warned by Rowley to expect fine words but no money.

- Joseph apologises that he is unable to help Stanley as Sir Oliver has given him nothing and he has spent his own money on his extravagant brother Charles.
- Sir Oliver declares under his breath that Charles will be his heir.
- Rowley returns to tell Joseph that Sir Oliver has arrived and will call shortly with Charles.

The scene is still Joseph's library, though the act curtain indicates the passage of a short period of time. Joseph reacts angrily to the news that Stanley has called, and in **soliloquy** tells the audience of his annoyance at having to put on appearances at a time when he has so many problems. He leaves the stage for a few moments and Rowley enters with Sir Oliver, who is pretending to be the poor relation Stanley. Rowley warns Sir Oliver that although Joseph will talk charitably, he will do nothing practical to help; for Joseph, '"Charity begins at home"', and does not extend beyond his own front door (lines 31–4). Joseph apologises that he is unable to help Stanley. When asked if he has had money from Sir Oliver, Joseph lies, saying he has received only a few trinkets – much to Sir Oliver's indignation, conveyed in an aside. In addition, Joseph claims to have spent so much on helping Charles that he has nothing left for his poor relation, so he sends Stanley away empty-handed. As he leaves, Sir Oliver tells the audience in another aside that Charles is now certain to have all his fortune.

Rowley brings the news that Sir Oliver has arrived from India and that he will be at Joseph's house, along with Charles, shortly. Joseph pretends to be delighted at the news but when on his own expresses his fear that his uncle will discover the truth about him as a result of the day's events.

COMMENTARY

This is another brief transitional scene following the high drama that has passed. Sheridan puts it to good use by showing Joseph continuing to practise his deceptions. The plot is now turning against him, however; the audience knows that by refusing to help 'Mr Stanley', Joseph is betraying himself to Sir Oliver and therefore

CONTEXT

Joseph's words, **'I wish you health and spirits'** (line 98), echo the New Testament: 'If a brother or sister be naked, and destitute of daily food, And one of you say unto them, Depart in peace, be ye warmed and filled; notwithstanding ye give them not those things which are needful to the body; what doth it profit?' (James 2:15–16). Joseph's empty words bring no 'profit' to Stanley, who leaves as poor as he arrived, whereas Charles, despite his disreputable lifestyle, actually gives something from the little money he has to help the man.

making it even more certain that he will be unmasked in the final scene.

Joseph, despite his weariness at having to play a part yet again in order to get rid of Stanley, continues to excel in his role, though the audience can probably detect the strain he is under by the excessive politeness he shows when Sir Oliver enters (see lines 40–1, 43–4). His finely balanced sentence in lines 87–8 is a good example of his skill with words: 'To pity without the power to relieve is still more painful than to ask and be denied.' This in fact means nothing more than 'this hurts me even more than it hurts you' and is in any case nonsense: it does not hurt Joseph one bit to send Stanley away empty-handed – in fact he reveals in his **soliloquy** in lines 102–8 that he knows full well he is offering 'sentimental French plate' – a cheap alternative to genuine charity – and he seems to enjoy telling us so. Stanley, for all Joseph knows, is in real distress and has nothing to live on, but Mr Surface has kept his own money safe.

The full depth of the stage at Drury Lane was again put to use at the end of the scene: as Rowley takes a long exit to the back of the stage, Joseph has to keep talking in double meanings and **asides** for five lines (122–8) until Rowley finally departs. Even his last few lines he has to divide between us and Rowley: 'I cannot express the sensations I feel at the thought of seeing him,' he says to Rowley, while confessing to us his true feeling that Sir Oliver's arrival is 'the cruellest piece of ill fortune' (lines 129–30). This doubling of Joseph's dialogue fits brilliantly with his depiction as a thoroughly duplicitous character.

QUESTION
What do you think this short scene adds to the play?

GLOSSARY

11	**policy** skill in managing affairs, pragmatism
25	**speculative** theoretical, professed
39	**complaisance** here, false congeniality
68	**pagodas** gold coins from India
70	**congou tea** a kind of black tea from China

70	avadavats Indian song-birds with red plumage, often kept as cagebirds
70–1	India crackers fireworks

SCENE 2

- The scandal school arrive at Sir Peter's house to find out the truth about the incident in Joseph's library.
- They each have their own sensational version of events; some involving a duel and serious injury to Sir Peter.
- Sir Peter enters; he is humiliated that the news is already all over the town and he drives them out of the house in a fury.
- He is further mortified when Sir Oliver reveals that he knows the whole story, though Sir Peter pretends to join Sir Oliver in laughing it off.
- Sir Oliver and Rowley urge Sir Peter to seek a reconciliation with Lady Teazle.

The scene is Sir Peter's house, where the scandal school arrive one by one to learn the full details of the incident in Joseph's library. The news has already been confused and inflated in a number of ways, so that they argue about which of the brothers was the lover and Sir Benjamin and Crabtree are convinced there was a duel in which Sir Peter was wounded, though they argue about whether it was with swords or pistols. Mistaking Sir Oliver for a doctor, they pester him for details; he is amused to introduce Sir Peter, fit and well, though wounded in his pride at the way the news has spread so fast and he is such a subject of mockery. He drives the gossips out of his house. Sir Oliver and Rowley tease Sir Peter by telling him he was right about the Surface brothers, turning back on him his praise of Joseph in the first two acts. He pretends to share their amusement as they refer to the events in the library, though he is clearly distressed. They leave him to attempt a reconciliation with Lady Teazle, who is in the adjoining room in tears, Rowley having

CONTEXT

Accounts of a duel would not have seemed fanciful to Sheridan's audience, even if these details are ridiculous. In 1807 Sheridan and John Colclough stood together for election in Wexford. In a duel over the ownership of votes on the last day of the poll, Colclough was shot dead by William Alcock, one of their opponents. Incredibly, Alcock was not only elected but also acquitted of murder, although he went mad and ended his days in a straightjacket.

reassured Sir Peter that a letter he found from Lady Teazle to Charles was a forgery designed to deceive him. They all return to Joseph's house for the final uncovering of hypocrisy.

COMMENTARY

Sheridan varies the tone again here, with the increasingly excited scandal school arguing noisily about the particulars of the scene at Joseph's house. This is the first time we have seen them since Act II; their malice has increased now that they have something truly scandalous to enjoy, especially as it involves people they know. Mrs Candour, true to form, fears she will not be able to spread the news of the misfortunes of her 'friends' very far before it is in the newspapers. Sheridan mocks their fantastic invention and pretended sympathy. Sir Benjamin and Crabtree provide the most detailed, but conflicting, descriptions of a duel that has never taken place – such as the bullet that 'struck against a little bronze Shakespeare ... and wounded the postman' (lines 88–90; we are even told where the letter came from and the postage!) Lady Sneerwell, however, is genuinely affected by the false reports – she cannot be pleased to hear that it was Charles who fought Sir Peter; however, if his name is cleared he will then be free to marry Maria. She leaves in some distress, to find 'better information' (line 95). Sir Oliver on the other hand remains a man of bluff good sense, enjoying being mistaken for a doctor before introducing Sir Peter 'walking as if nothing at all was the matter' (lines 130–1).

Once the scandalmongers have been driven out of the house the tone softens. Sheridan has finished exposing the true cruelty of Lady Sneerwell's set (though she herself will make a brief appearance in the final scene) and the play needs to take a more kindly turn. Sir Oliver and Rowley joke in a friendly way about Sir Peter's foolish trust in Joseph's sentiments, then the mention of a truly repentant Lady Teazle and the possibility of a reconciliation introduces an emotional note. Sheridan continues his transformation of Sir Peter into a more sympathetic character; although he wonders whether to let Lady Teazle suffer a little longer (line 231) he has no desire to triumph over her in the way we

QUESTION

How does Sheridan vary the pace in this scene? Look at the characters' entrances and exits for some clues.

have previously seen. 'What a remarkably elegant turn of the head she has!' (lines 238–9), he remarks and is soon talking of their being 'the happiest couple in the country' (line 247). Although this is another example of Sir Peter's sudden changes of mood, a happy outcome can surely no longer be in doubt.

GLOSSARY

8	**at length** the names printed in the newspapers in full, not just the initials (as in the Prologue, line 14)
19	**Mr Surface is the gallant** Joseph, as the elder brother, is 'Mr Surface'; a 'gallant' is a lover
61	**hartshorn** another word for *sal volatile* (Prologue, line 15)
68	**thrust in second** a fencing term for a thrust under the opponent's sword, with the knuckles upward
91	**double letter** a letter written on two sheets, and therefore charged double postage
101	**deny him** deny that he (Sir Peter) is in the house
103	**the faculty** the medical profession
110	**for a hundred** Crabtree is willing to bet £100 that his version of the story is true
138–9	**without law or physic** without either lawyers or doctors being involved (a reference to the way these professions profit from death by providing expensive, and by implication, ineffectual medicines and managing the affairs after death)
139	**these gentlemen … killed you** they would have killed him metaphorically, i.e. spread the story of his death
166	**high** loud, angry
224	**discovering** revealing

CONTEXT

The term **'the Montem'** (line 82) comes from the Montem Mound ('montem' is Latin for mountain), also called Salt Hill, an ancient mound of earth near the town of Slough in Berkshire. It was traditional for a procession of schoolboys from the nearby public school, Eton, to walk to the mound, collecting money on the way to pay the Senior Scholar's expenses at King's College, Cambridge. The practice was abolished in 1847.

SCENE THE LAST (3)

- Lady Sneerwell and Joseph plan how to make the best of their present situation.
- Sir Oliver enters and, taking him for Stanley, Joseph tries to get rid of him. As he is pushing him out of the room, Charles arrives.
- Charles also wants rid of the man he believes to be Mr Premium before Sir Oliver arrives, and joins his brother in forcing Sir Oliver to the door just as Sir Peter, Lady Teazle, Maria and Rowley arrive.
- The brothers realise their mistake, after which Sir Oliver, Sir Peter and Lady Teazle all denounce Joseph; Sir Oliver forgives Charles.
- Maria says she believes Charles is committed to Lady Sneerwell rather than to her.
- Lady Sneerwell re-enters, expecting Snake to support her lies but he has been paid double to tell the truth.
- Charles and Maria will be married the next morning and all ends happily.

CONTEXT

Sheridan wrote the play with specific actors at Drury Lane in mind. He originally intended Maria to be played by Mrs Robinson, but she was pregnant and too 'unshaped', so the part was taken by Priscilla Hopkins, the prompter's daughter. Sheridan later told a friend that he had not written a love scene for Charles and Maria because the actors were not suitable; this may also explain why she has so small a part.

The final scene takes place in Joseph's library. Lady Sneerwell reproaches Joseph bitterly for chasing after Lady Teazle instead of being satisfied with Maria. Joseph assures her that some forged love-letters supposed to be between her and Charles can be used to retain her hold on his brother. At the sound of knocking, she retires to an adjoining room. Joseph is angered by Sir Oliver's entrance; still believing him to be Mr Stanley, Joseph does not want him to meet his uncle and reveal his own miserly behaviour. As he is attempting to force Sir Oliver out, Charles enters and, taking Sir Oliver for the broker, tries to defend 'Mr Premium' from his brother. However, he too realises that a meeting between this man and his uncle would be unfortunate and is helping Joseph eject Sir Oliver when they are interrupted by Sir Peter, Lady Teazle, Maria and Rowley. The brothers realise their mistake and turn to each other in amazement. Joseph is denounced by Sir Oliver, Sir Peter and Lady Teazle in turn.

Charles expects a worse fate but is forgiven by his uncle; unlike Joseph he is genuinely pleased to see Sir Oliver. It seems as though the way is clear for Charles to marry Maria but she sadly declares that he is already committed to someone else. Joseph ushers in Lady Sneerwell who accuses Charles of disloyalty to her, expecting Snake to support her story about the forged love-letters. Snake has however been paid more to reveal the truth. Lady Teazle resigns from the 'scandalous college' (line 187) and Lady Sneerwell leaves in a fury, followed by Joseph. Snakes begs that they will keep his good deed secret to protect his reputation. Charles and Maria are now reunited and Sir Oliver declares that they will be married the next morning. With Sir Peter and Lady Teazle also reconciled, the play ends happily with a few lines of verse from Charles, first to Maria and then to the audience.

CONTEXT

The phrase **'my little broker'** (line 60) is one of several references to Richard Yates, the original Sir Oliver, who was a small man.

COMMENTARY

Joseph's library is the appropriate setting for the final revelations, for it was here in the 'screen scene' that his plotting was first uncovered. Sheridan rounds off the plot with some skill, ensuring that each of the major players gets their just deserts. Although Joseph and Lady Sneerwell make one last attempt to disrupt events, the bitterness with which they accuse each other indicates that they no longer have any real power. When Sir Oliver is revealed, Joseph and Charles receive the verdicts they are due; for Charles this results in a very handsome reward. The return of Lady Sneerwell brings a brief threat to the triumph of love. However, Snake has, true to form, changed sides again (as hinted earlier, see III.1.39–42). Joseph and Lady Sneerwell are forced to retire defeated and the happy couples now take centre stage for the final curtain.

Sheridan gives each of his characters the opportunity to demonstrate their particular traits. Lady Sneerwell is furious, for her feelings are hurt, whilst Joseph, although temporarily silenced when confronted by Sir Oliver in his true guise, persists in his deceptions to the very last, pretending in his final lines that he is seeking to protect his brother, despite have done everything in his power to harm him. As Sir Peter says, he is 'Moral to the last drop!' (lines 200–3). Sir Oliver also neatly sums up these two figures as 'oil and vinegar' (lines 204). Unlike his brother, Charles makes no pretence that he can justify himself, his honesty standing in direct contrast to Joseph's guile. He is as good natured as earlier, jesting with Sir Oliver about '*family secrets*' (that is, the sale of the portraits, line 128) and pinpoints his essentially redeemable character with: 'If I do not appear mortified at the exposure of my follies, it is because I feel at this moment the warmest satisfaction in seeing you, my liberal benefactor' (lines 140–2). He makes no promises to reform, 'and that I take to be a proof that I intend to set about it' (lines 243–4); in other words, there is far more faith to be had in unpretentious realism, however unsaintly, than hollow promises. Sir Oliver has been justified in his test of the brothers and in his faith in Charles, despite Sir Peter's trust in Joseph.

Lady Teazle demonstrates her change of heart by announcing that she no longer 'kills characters' (lines 190); instead she is the first to seek to bring Charles and Maria together in this scene (lines 146–7) and sees Lady Sneerwell's 'curse' of fifty years with Sir Peter as a blessing (lines 191–2). Sir Peter is a happy man again; no longer afraid of Lady Sneerwell's tongue, he mocks her fury in line 193, and can jest about his own troubles in the earlier scenes by saying to the young couple, 'may you live as happily together as Lady Teazle and I – intend to do!' (lines 234–5).

QUESTION

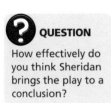

How effectively do you think Sheridan brings the play to a conclusion?

Sheridan keeps the action moving quickly and the tone light. Joseph and Lady Sneerwell are almost pantomime villains now, with only the show of power, and do not long cloud the overall romantic, even sentimental, atmosphere (Sir Peter tells Maria: 'speak your sentiments!', line 150). Although he has disposed of the scandal school, Sheridan wants to bring all the other major characters together for the final scene, but ensures that a quick succession of entrances and exits keep the action moving. The arrival of Sir Oliver leads each brother to mistake him for one of the fictitious characters he has played, and their comic attempt to force him out is the most physical moment in the play. This is cleverly followed at once by the stunned immobility of the brothers as they realise who he is (lines 95–8). Joseph's denunciation is in the form of triple accusations, to which he has no immediate reply (lines 99–112). Charles is more jocular when the spotlight is turned on him, sidling up to his uncle to ask him to keep the '*family secrets*'. Through this, Sheridan implies his crimes are essentially the harmless follies of youth, and, crucially, Charles has done nothing to undermine the family, unlike Joseph who harmed both his brother and poor Mr Stanley. Maria, a rather passive romantic heroine, has few lines; her role is mainly to be admired and praised by Charles, particularly in the final verse (lines 247–50). Snake has a brief role in the final stage of the plot, turning his treachery to vindicate the good, but comically not wishing to ruin his bad reputation (lines 215–18). With real virtue triumphant, Charles steps forward to invite the audience's approval in the traditional way with a couplet at the end of the scene.

CHECK THE FILM

The 1988 film *Dangerous Liaisons* (dir. Stephen Frears) is based on Pierre Choderlos de Laclos' novel *Les Liaisons Dangereuses* (1782), a story of scheming, deception and infidelity among the French aristocracy. The film is visually stunning with period costumes and settings.

GLOSSARY

4	Can passion furnish a remedy? Can being angry help you?
16	bate hold back
40	diffidence doubt
43	baited harassed, persecuted
75	A. B. the initials used when leaving a message at the coffee-house, to hide one's identity: Charles implies that Stanley goes by a number of aliases
219	traduce misrepresent

EPILOGUE

- The actor who has played Lady Teazle concludes the play with a farewell to her fashionable life in London.
- She imagines the dull country existence Lady Teazle will face.
- The playwright advises all ladies to follow Lady Teazle's example and shun vice in real life.

The Epilogue, like the Prologue the work of another writer, has Lady Teazle invite the audience to imagine her quiet country life as

CONTEXT

The Epilogue was written by George Colman the Elder (1732–94), like Sheridan, a playwright and theatre manager.

she and Sir Peter leave the fashionable, but corrupt, world of London behind. There is ambivalence both in her regret at leaving her life of fashion and in her description of the unrefined, pastoral life she will inherit. The final words are given to the playwright as he urges the moral of the play and silences Lady Teazle's complaints.

COMMENTARY

There are echoes here of the description Lady Teazle gives in Act II Scene 1 of her dull existence before she married Sir Peter and adopted London ways (see II.1.37–46). Colman describes her future in rather melodramatic terms: she is 'untimely blasted in her bloom' and, condemned to 'dismal doom' (lines 17–8) – the verse is almost doggerel at this point. The long series of 'farewells' in lines 32–42 is a comic **parody** of Othello's farewell to his military profession. The Epilogue ends on a sententious note with the advice to women to avoid vice and folly.

CHECK THE BOOK

See *Othello*, III.3.349–58. What in Shakespeare's play was tragic, prompted by his wife's supposed infidelity, is here comic: the battles are only card games.

This moral note perhaps jars slightly with the play itself, just as the verse has a more ponderous feel than Sheridan's light dialogue. Although Lady Teazle has given up 'her follies' (line 48), she does so with wit and grace, in response to her husband (and her own conscience, we assume). It is not easy to imagine her settling so quickly back into the dull life of an old country wife described here. That may be the point: as Mrs Abington was a famous comic actor it would be easy for her to suggest an **ironic** tone throughout this final speech.

CONTEXT

Members of Sheridan's audience who read the *Town and Country Magazine* would have known that Mrs Abington was the mistress of Lord Shelbourne, so would have seen a certain irony in her recommending the strict moral code of the conclusion to this Epilogue.

GLOSSARY

5	**virtuous bard** Sheridan; he has commended the virtues of marriage and morality in the play
	motley Bayes motley is a jester's multicoloured costume; Bayes is the name of the playwright in Buckingham's comedy *The Rehearsal* of 1672 (the name is taken from the bay laurel, sprigs of which were woven into a wreath of leaves to crown a conqueror or poet in classical antiquity)
28	**loo** a card game
28	**vole** winning all the tricks in card games such as ombre

29	**'Seven's the main!'** a call in hazard (gambling with dice): main is the winning number called out
30	**hot cockles** a game, often played at Christmas, where a blindfolded player has to guess who has struck them
36	**Spadille** ace of spades (in the games ombre and quadrille)
36	**pam** jack of clubs (in the game loo, the highest-scoring card)
36	**basto** ace of clubs (in the games quadrille and ombre)

EXTENDED COMMENTARIES

TEXT 1 – ACT I SCENE 1, LINES 1–172

During the course of this opening scene Sheridan does more than simply introduce the plot and many of his main characters. The play begins with the discussion of intrigue and it soon becomes clear that deception and hypocrisy will play a significant part in what is to follow.

The dialogue of this scene is full of references to deception: 'a feigned hand', 'suspicion' and 'intrigue' occur in the first four lines. In fact the majority of the dialogue in the early part of this scene is characterised by a sardonic, bitter edge; only with the arrival of Mrs Candour about halfway through the scene does the mockery become lighter in tone as a result of her garrulous gossip. Sheridan's audience would have immediately recognised the word 'paragraphs' in the first line as a reference to the planting of malicious stories in the newspapers – and this is in any case made explicit by Snake's mention of the *Town and Country Magazine* in lines 17–18. The language used by Lady Sneerwell and Snake reveals their moral standards: the rumour about Lady Brittle and Captain Boastall is 'in as fine a train as your ladyship could wish', 'Mrs Clackitt has a very pretty talent' and 'has been tolerably successful' (lines 6–12). Couched in the language of politeness and virtue, success as a slanderer, we are told, is measured by the engagements broken off, heirs disinherited and divorces brought about by rumour and deception. Sheridan's **satiric** purpose is clearly implied in these

CONTEXT

Sheridan probably based Snake on a character called Dr Viper in Samuel Foote's *The Capuchin* of 1776. Foote's character was widely assumed to be a portrait of the Irish clergyman and journalist William Jackson, editor of the *Public Ledger* and a notorious spreader of salacious gossip.

opening lines, as he reveals to the audience the vices that he will attack during the course of the play.

Lady Sneerwell is an ideal focus for Sheridan's exploration of the contrast between appearance and reality in this scene. As a representative of London society (Snake informs us that she is 'the widow of a City knight, with a good jointure' in lines 48–9), Lady Sneerwell governs her life by a perverse moral code in which she claims to be 'no hypocrite' when she enjoys the 'success' of her destructive rumours (lines 30–1). Her own sufferings from 'the envenomed tongue of slander' (lines 32–3), rather than allowing her to sympathise with victims of gossip, have caused her to seek to ruin the reputation of as many people as she can. It seems that 'reducing others to [her] level' (line 34) is the only satisfaction she can get.

Sheridan continues to focus on hypocrisy as the scene progresses. The conversation between Lady Sneerwell and Snake from line 40 does more than merely inform the audience about the Surface brothers; it also develops Sheridan's exposure of the shallowness of reputation and the prevalence of deception. If Joseph is 'universally well spoken of', and 'passes for a youthful miracle of prudence, good sense, and benevolence', this merely confirms his hypocrisy and the poor judgement of society (and of the gullible Sir Peter in particular) for Joseph, who is held to be a 'Man of Sentiment', is in fact 'a sentimental knave' (lines 73–7). 'Sentiment' will be a key term in this play and the audience is warned early on that Sheridan sees it as a cover for duplicity. In addition, when Lady Sneerwell uses the term 'moral' to describe Joseph, she does so as an insult: Joseph has forgotten that 'among friends' (that is, in corrupt society) morality in the conventional sense has no place (lines 109–10).

The very names of some of the characters make Sheridan's purposes clear: the audience can expect Lady Sneerwell and Sir Benjamin Backbite to be satirical creations designed to portray a distinctive but narrow range of behaviour. As the elder brother, Joseph is identified in the text as 'Surface' and that is all he is; his pretended morality is only for public consumption: 'I'll keep that sentiment till I see Sir Peter,' he says in line 111. By allowing us to see Joseph talking like this in private, Sheridan makes sure that we, unlike

CONTEXT

The phrase, **'Man of Sentiment'** (line 77), follows the pattern of titles of the period, such as John Lee's play *The Man of Quality* (1773) and Henry Mackenzie's popular novel *The Man of Feeling* (1771).Through Joseph, Sheridan **satirises** the exaggerated form that expressions of sentiment, or moral feelings, had come to take in the period. By turning sentiment to hypocrisy – Lady Sneerwell describes Joseph as **'a sentimental knave'** (line 73) – **ironically** contrasting his professed morals with his real malice, Sheridan suggests that the emotional outpourings and heightened moral senses so popular in contemporary culture are likewise a sham.

Sir Peter, know his real nature from the start. In the same way, Joseph makes the significance of Snake's name unmistakable: like the serpent in the Garden of Eden, '[he] hasn't enough virtue to be faithful even to his own villainy' (lines 128–9). Later events confirm Joseph's suspicions when he betrays Joseph and Lady Sneerwell in the final scene. Amusingly, Snake seems to find this uncharacteristic good deed rather embarrassing and is eager to retain his bad name – in this corrupt society a reputation for deception is clearly an important guarantee of income.

The reference to 'Maria's heart' (line 81), hints that there may be a place for more genuine sentiments in the play, though it is clear that Lady Sneerwell will do all she can to oppose this love. Already in this opening scene, Sheridan is using the appearance of Maria as an opportunity to emphasise the moral contrasts on which his **satire** depends. To Maria, Sir Benjamin is 'disagreeable' and his uncle 'odious'; she denounces their gossip as 'perpetual libel', 'malice' and 'contemptible' rather than 'witty' conversation and mere 'raillery', as Joseph and Lady Sneerwell prefer to term it (lines 131–56). Maria also provides a moral judgement on Mrs Candour, who has only a 'very gross affectation of good nature and benevolence' and not genuine feeling (line 168). While extravagant professions of benevolence imply hypocrisy, there is nevertheless a need for a real moral counterweight to expose the duplicity in the play. It seems that Maria, and in part, Charles, are the characters to do this; she with her natural and unaffected innocence and he with the cheerful disposition and good-hearted generosity that will emerge later in the play.

TEXT 2 – ACT IV SCENE 1

This scene marks a moral turning point in the play, as it is the point at which Charles secures the affection of his uncle and therefore ensures that he will be rescued from the results of his extravagance by Sir Oliver's money. His victory is perhaps deliberately constructed by Sheridan to come not from the scheme devised by Sir Oliver to test the brothers – their response to the request to help a poor relation – but from an instinctive affection for his uncle's portrait (and therefore for the man himself). Charles' generosity in the former respect follows at the end of this scene; once he has

CONTEXT

In at least one manuscript copy of the play, Charles says when he picks up the family genealogy at line 18: 'What parchment have we here? Richard, heir to Thomas ...'. This was presumably a family joke, as Richard Brinsley Sheridan was indeed the son of Thomas and now taking on his mantle as a theatre manager. However, Richard was the second son; his elder brother, Charles, was always his father's favourite though he was, by all accounts, more like Joseph Surface than the Charles of the play.

secured payment for the paintings he immediately sends money to Mr Stanley. Sheridan has already given the audience plenty of opportunities to observe Joseph's hypocrisies and needs now to show Charles' true character.

CONTEXT

The prodigal son is a parable in the New Testament (Luke 15:11–32, often called the 'lost son' in modern translations). In the parable the younger son asks for his share of the inheritance and squanders it; when poverty brings him to his senses he returns home to seek forgiveness. His father throws a party in celebration but the elder son is so angry at this that he will not join in. The parallels with the two brothers in the play are clear, though of course their father has already died.

As often in this play, the audience is aware of far more than Sheridan permits his characters on stage to know. By the end of the previous scene, the audience has heard Charles talk freely of being the 'prodigious favourite' of his uncle, not realising that he is actually talking to the man himself (III.3.151–2). Charles' carelessness about selling the portraits seems to threaten his future, since we realise that Sir Oliver begins to take this as an insult to the family. 'Oh, the prodigal!' he cries in an **aside** (III.3.236). However, it seems that like the prodigal son in the Gospel parable, Charles will be accepted back into the family whilst his ungenerous older brother will be censured. Like the biblical prodigal, Charles has squandered almost all his father's money, though the alert listener will have noticed that Charles had shown a little more familial affection when he bought his father's home from his elder brother. Sir Oliver condemns Joseph's action in selling the house as 'reprehensible' (III.2.12), a reminder that he will judge by actions rather than words, as he declared earlier that he would 'make a trial of their hearts' (II.3.66).

So it is to prove; although Sir Oliver's commentary on the sale indicates that he laments Charles' thoughtless disposal of his ancestors, he takes the affectionate loyalty to his own portrait as a sign of a generous and good heart. It is clear that Sir Oliver is a man of feeling, though not in the hypocritical sense that Joseph demonstrates. It is possible that, as a younger son himself, Sheridan was commenting on the difference between the assumed supremacy of the older son (known as primogeniture) and true virtue. Charles has no concern, it seems, for his ancestors since he gives the parchment of the genealogy to Careless to use as a hammer in the auction: 'you may knock down my ancestors with their own pedigree' (lines 21–2), implying that the family tree is in effect a 'catalogue' of social hierarchy rather than a documentation of real character and true family values. Certainly, in the play the younger son wins the rewards through his innate goodness rather than because of the accident of being born first; as Sir Oliver comments in an aside, 'How like his father the dog is!' (line 109). Sheridan, like many in the growing middle-class audience, sought to make his way in the world on the basis of his own skills and merits rather than because of his family background – an increasing source of tension during this period, as pressure for reform grew in Britain, stimulated by examples in America and France, but opposed by the establishment (see **Historical background**).

This scene was considered sufficiently important for Sheridan to have a special back flat painted showing the family portraits. Charles' high-spirited dialogue allows Sheridan to mock old fashioned portraiture – and slip in a few words of praise for his friend Sir Joshua Reynolds, who had already painted both Richard and Elizabeth Sheridan. In part this follows a familiar pattern of amusement at the expense of changing styles and fashions in both painting and dress, such as the pastoral scene with 'great-aunt Deborah ... a shepherdess feeding her flock' (lines 41–3). Sheridan adds a **satirical** comment, too, on the contrast between earlier fashion 'when beaux wore wigs, and the ladies their own hair' – a contrast to the excessively tall wigs worn by fashionable women in the late 1770s (lines 49–50) – and on Members of Parliament being 'bought and sold' (line 67), something about which, as an aspiring MP himself, Sheridan would have been acutely aware. Charles continues his banter with the pictures even after Sir Oliver has left, thanking them, in a theatrical gesture, as 'Ladies and gentlemen' – we can imagine his comic bow to the paintings (line 143). The scene ends with Charles sending £100 to Stanley, an impulsive action that Rowley advises him is against his own interests – he should first pay off his own debts. However, the audience know that Rowley will report to Sir Oliver that Charles has now already passed the second test by demonstrating his generous heart. As Charles remarks, **ironically** unaware how prophetic he is being, 'But I shall be rich and splenetic all in good time' (lines 150–1). It is, however, hard to image Sheridan's perpetually high-spirited young hero ever being 'splenetic'.

CONTEXT

The phrase, **'this is the first time they were ever bought and sold'** (lines 66–7), suggests that when employed as Members of Parliament William and Walter Blunt had not taken bribes, in a time when politics was notoriously corrupt and MPs were often under the control of a patron. Sheridan himself, who was elected in 1780, refused several offers of positions in government in order to maintain his independence.

CONTEXT

At their peak, ladies' hairstyles could extend as much as three feet above the head, with an elaborate headdress on top.

> **CONTEXT**
>
> The phrase, 'an absolute Joseph' (line 233), is a reference to the story in the Old Testament (Genesis 39) of Joseph who, as a slave, resisted the advances of his master's wife, finally fleeing from the house only to be falsely accused of attempting to rape her. There is a double **irony** here: Joseph Surface is quite the reverse of the biblical hero, attempting to seduce his patron's wife, and he is also not the 'absolute Joseph' Surface he pretends to be in public.

TEXT 3 – ACT IV SCENE 3

The audience, having seen Charles win the heart of his uncle in the previous two scenes, is likely to expect the action to move towards a climax as his brother becomes the focus of attention. Even before Sir Oliver can test Joseph's response to Stanley's poverty, however, the elder brother is exposed by the excesses of his own scheming. Sheridan displays this vividly through the actions on stage, as a succession of visitors increase the pressure on Joseph until all is revealed by the overthrow of the screen. If the scenes at Charles' house were **sentimental** in tone, the atmosphere is now one of **farce**, in which the actions become improbably complicated. In the tradition of farce, action is dominant as characters hide and are discovered – this is the one scene in *The School for Scandal* that relies to any extent on rapid activity and the physical representation of deception. The audience's amusement derives from the knowledge that Joseph is constantly on the verge of discovery and disaster. It is a tribute to Sheridan's skill that he sustains Joseph's precarious position for over 350 lines before bringing down the screen that the audience has been watching since Lady Teazle first cowered behind it.

In order for the exposure of Joseph to have the greatest impact, Sheridan brings together the key players one by one. First, the audience observes Lady Teazle, whom we have seen so far practising the art of scandal and demonstrating her superior powers over her infatuated husband, now faced with a far more dangerous adversary. Joseph, as the audience knows, is a hypocrite who seeks only to take advantage of Lady Teazle; Sheridan reminds us of this in his words to the audience just before she arrives: 'I wish I may not lose the heiress, through the scrape I have drawn myself in with the wife' (lines 4–6). Whilst Sheridan's audience would not tolerate the portrayal of real immorality on stage, they were keenly aware of the importance of reputation, especially for women. Through malicious scandal a woman could lose her reputation even if her virtue was in reality still intact, and without her reputation she could no longer move in fashionable society. This power made scandal both so attractive and so dangerous. Joseph's suggestion that in order to preserve her faultless reputation Lady Teazle should commit a 'minor' indiscretion (lines 69–77) is therefore genuinely disturbing advice. However, he is allowed to tempt Lady Teazle with his false logic just far enough for her virtue to appear to be in real danger before the servant interrupts with news of Sir Peter's arrival. Lady Teazle's alarm reveals the seriousness of her situation, but it is also comic. Her repetition of 'I'm ruined! I'm ruined!' is melodramatic and her term 'Mr Logic' is a sarcastic reminder of Joseph's smooth-tongued deception (lines 99–102).

Sir Peter's arrival is the first of three carefully timed, if improbable, interruptions. Each threatens to bring about Joseph's downfall – Sir Peter by his generosity to his wife and his talk of Maria, Charles by his rash words, and the anonymous 'person come on particular business' (line 327) by leaving the three characters alone on stage without Joseph present to prevent disaster. The audience is likely to relish the prospect of the anticipated unmasking of Joseph yet also to want to enjoy watching him prolong the deception for as long as possible. The screen itself is a visual reminder to the audience of the ever-present possibility of discovery in the scene. It is placed prominently in the centre of the stage – and almost immediately Sir Peter goes over to it, increasing the tension by the possibility he may look behind it. Sheridan underlines this through the dialogue. When Sir Peter comments, 'you make even your screen a source of knowledge – hung, I perceive with maps', Joseph's reply that he finds 'great use in that screen' is full of **dramatic irony**. Joseph and the audience know that, as he says in an **aside**, he has hidden something there 'in a hurry' and we expect that the screen itself, rather than the maps, will be a 'source of knowledge' for Sir Peter before the scene is out (lines 111–16).

> **QUESTION**
> How does Sheridan maintain the tension in this long scene? It might help you to chart the entrances, exits and movements on the stage.

The farce continues as the old husband confides his woes to Joseph whilst Joseph's comments are an ironic counterpoint. Joseph can hardly be 'very sorry to hear' that Lady Teazle has made Sir Peter unhappy (line 125), nor astonished that she appears to have found a lover – so his apparently sympathetic responses are in fact comic, especially when Sir Peter says he believes he knows the man involved. Joseph's 'alarm' stems, we know, not from sympathy but from fear of discovery – and Sheridan loads on more comic innuendo when Joseph says 'such a discovery would hurt me just as much as it would you' – as events will indeed prove (lines 131–4). The tension relaxes slightly when Joseph learns that Sir Peter suspects Charles, and he even manages to construct one of his 'sentiments', winning Sir Peter's praise. Again, the audience see the **irony**: we 'never hear [Charles] talk so' because Charles is not a hypocrite (lines 145–6). Joseph recovers some composure for the next few speeches, responding to each of Sir Peter's laments with carefully composed sympathetic remarks that are, nevertheless, heavy with irony as the behaviour he is professing to condemn is, of course, his own. Joseph's duplicity reaches a climax in a speech of high-flown rhetoric culminating in an artfully balanced sentence: 'However, if it should be proved on him, he is no longer a brother of mine; I disclaim kindred with him; for the man who can break the laws of hospitality and attempt the wife of his friend, deserves to be branded as the pest of society' (lines 171–5). Sir Peter imagines that this is a description of Charles, but we know as well as Joseph that it is the elder brother who is the 'pest'. Sir Peter's praise of these 'noble sentiments' is another reminder that Sheridan almost always uses the word 'sentiments' ironically – later in the scene Charles will be able to mock: 'Sir Peter, there's nothing in the world so noble as a Man of Sentiment!' (lines 376–7).

Sheridan changes the pace again when Sir Peter explains the arrangements he proposes for Lady Teazle's financial independence. As the conversation turns to Maria, Joseph becomes increasingly agitated in his attempts to change the subject; Sheridan's repetition of '*softly*' in the stage directions (lines 198–201) indicates Joseph's desperation as he attempts to silence Sir Peter without being heard by Lady Teazle. The arrival of the servant introduces further complications but also provides a brief distraction for Sir Peter. In the tradition of **farce**, Sheridan piles one absurdity on another when Sir Peter seeks to hide to spy on Charles and in the process glimpses 'a petticoat' behind the screen (line 229). It seems inevitable that Joseph will now be caught out; instead, Sheridan allows him to keep discovery at bay a little longer by a further deception, which has Sir Peter seek refuge behind one of the doors at the side of the stage. With husband and wife peeping out from their hiding places to reinforce the comic absurdity of the situation, Sheridan exercises his

CONTEXT

Garrick, Sheridan's predecessor as manager of Drury Lane, continued to take a kindly interest in the theatre. He wrote to Sheridan a few days after the first performance: 'A gentleman who is as mad as myself about ye School remark'd, that the characters upon the stage at ye falling of the screen stand too long before they speak; – I thought so too the first night ... – tho' they should be astonish'd, and a little petrify'd, yet it may be carry'd to too great a length' (cited in Kelly, *Richard Brinsley Sheridan: A Life*, p. 80).

skills by giving Joseph lines that will satisfy both Charles and his hidden listeners.

Joseph's situation is becoming impossible, however, as his various intrigues become entangled and out of control. Charles begins to tease his brother about Lady Teazle and Joseph resorts to the desperate measure of revealing the presence of Sir Peter. Although this allows a warm-hearted reconciliation between Sir Peter and Charles, Joseph's respite is short-lived; another visitor allows enough time for Sir Peter to reveal the presence of the 'little French milliner' (line 355) and, with a final burst of physical action, a tussle brings down the screen. For once, as Charles says, 'morality' (that is, hypocrisy) is 'dumb' (line 371). After all the action and expectation of a **denouement**, the stunned silence is an effective theatrical device, as realisation dawns on Sir Peter, Lady Teazle is too ashamed to speak and Joseph is confounded. Although Joseph recovers enough to attempt an explanation, his stammering performance indicates that he is defeated and Sheridan ensures that when he does begin one of his 'sentiments' at the end of the scene he is not allowed to complete the sentence.

QUESTION

Examine the comic use of double meanings in this scene.

Part Three

Critical approaches

> **CONTEXT**
> E. M. Forster (1879–1970) is best known for his novels *Howards End* (1910) and *A Passage to India* (1924). The lectures printed as *Aspects of the Novel* form an accessible introduction to the art of fiction.

Characterisation

Sheridan, writing for the accomplished actors at Drury Lane, created a series of well-defined characters in *The School for Scandal*. Even small parts, such as Trip, are sharply delineated and the author's skill in characterisation repays careful study.

E. M. Forster distinguished between 'flat' and 'round' characters – that is between 'types' who have one distinguishing feature and three-dimensional figures who feel more convincingly human. Forster adds that flat people 'are best when they are comic ... It is only round people who are fit to perform tragically for any length of time and who can move us to any feelings except humour' (*Aspects of the Novel*, Penguin, 1927, Chapter 4). Comedy and melodrama usually rely on a series of flat, stock characters such as the jealous old husband, the flighty young wife and so on. Some of Sheridan's characters clearly fall into the 'flat' category, with names like Careless and Backbite; others have more complex characterisation.

Sir Peter Teazle

Sheridan created Sir Peter along the familiar lines of the ageing husband struggling to cope with a much younger wife. 'Lady Teazle made me the happiest of men – and I have been the miserablest dog' (I.2.2–3). His blindness to his own weaknesses is used to comic effect; he describes himself as 'the sweetest-tempered man alive' yet he argues with his wife 'a hundred times a day' (I.2.28–30). The furious quarrels in Act II Scene 1 and Act III Scene 1 are magnificent set pieces in which he is the victim of his wife's quicker wit and better self-control – but also, Sheridan seems to imply, it is his genuine love for his wife that puts him in her power. His most affectionate comments tend to be uttered when she is just off-stage, such as: 'How happy I should be if I could tease her into loving me, though but a little' (III.1.166–7), showing the difficulty he has in communicating his feelings to his dauntingly spirited spouse. These details, together with his compassionate actions later in the play, make him a more rounded character than merely 'a stiff, peevish old bachelor ... who might be my father' as Lady Teazle so rudely describes him (III.1.196–8).

Sir Peter's gullibility extends to his estimation of the Surface brothers; we know of Joseph's hypocrisy from the first scene but Sir Peter is still defending him right up to his exposure in the 'screen scene' of Act IV. He is tyrannical in his treatment of Maria, his ward; having made his mind up about the Surface brothers he forbids her to see Charles and wishes to compel her to marry Joseph against her will. However, Sheridan allows his character to become more human once he has seen the folly of his ways in the 'screen scene' – and learnt that Lady Teazle might be reconciled with him. When the scandal school arrive at his house, eager for news, he is no longer afraid of any damage they might do; the audience will surely be glad that he abruptly throws them out of the house. Sheridan ensures that he remains true to character by showing him to be as convinced of his future happiness as he was of his former misery, though perhaps he has gained a greater ability to laugh at himself when he says to Maria and Charles, 'may you live together as happily as Lady Teazle and I – intend to do!' (V.3.234–5).

LADY TEAZLE

Although Sheridan tells us that Lady Teazle has only been married to Sir Peter and living in London for six months, he portrays her as an accomplished member of fashionable society. She has none of the comic rustic ignorance of Bob Acres in *The Rivals*, though her 'country prejudices' (II.2.231) make her hesitate about entering into a relationship with Joseph (see IV.3.88–93). She has, however, learnt enough from Lady Sneerwell and her companions to join in their slanders, though with rather less malice. Her name may be the clue: Lady Teazle's delight is in teasing, especially when her husband responds so readily to whatever she says.

Sheridan's real skill, however, is in creating such a high-spirited opponent for Sir Peter. In each of their quarrel scenes she is able to charm him and defeat him as she pleases; she knows that he is

CONTEXT

Frances Abington (1737–1815) was the finest comic actress of the time and had excelled playing both fine ladies and country girls – Lady Teazle's part combines both. Although Lady Teazle is supposedly much younger than her husband, Mrs Abington was forty in 1777, while Thomas King who played Sir Peter was forty-seven.

completely in her power. Sheridan provides her with some delightful ripostes to her choleric husband. When Sir Peter says, 'Zounds, madam, you had no taste when you married me', she is able to turn this immediately to her advantage: 'That's very true indeed, Sir Peter. After having married you I should never pretend to taste again, I allow', before leaving in high spirits for Lady Sneerwell's (II.1.76–80). She ends their second quarrel on an equally taunting note: 'Well, you are going to be in a passion, I see, and I shall only interrupt you; so bye, bye!' (III.1.254–5).

By the end of the play, Sheridan has allowed her to see the error of her ways – or more accurately, perhaps, of London society's ways. She has taken the side of honest plain speaking, saying of Joseph: 'I behold him now in a light so truly despicable that I shall never again respect myself for having listened to him' (IV.3.415–17). We are asked to believe that the difference in age is no longer a problem, as both Teazles have mellowed: 'she kills characters no longer' (V.3.190) and welcomes Lady Sneerwell's curse ('May your husband live these fifty years', V.3.191–2). This is in complete contrast to her earlier wish to be his widow (II.1.59–62).

LADY SNEERWELL

QUESTION

How convincing a villain is Lady Sneerwell? Do you think an audience would consider her a credible rival to Maria for the love of Charles?

As leader of the scandal school, Lady Sneerwell would appear to be cast as the most accomplished and malicious gossip in the play – as her name implies. Snake certainly praises her skills in such terms, referring to 'that delicacy of hint and mellowness of sneer which distinguishes your ladyship's scandal' (I.1.23–4). Her name links her with other two-dimensional members of the scandal school such as Mrs Candour and Sir Benjamin Backbite, but Sheridan gives Lady Sneerwell a little more complexity. Unlike the other members of the crew, she (like Joseph) spreads gossip for her own ends and not merely from general malice. 'I am no hypocrite to deny the satisfaction I reap from the success of my efforts,' she says (I.1.30–1), but also confesses that it is for Charles' sake that she is 'thus anxious and malicious' (I.1.67). Out of her professed love for Charles she does all she can to prevent his union with Maria. She blackens Charles' character so that Sir Peter will be prejudiced against him, and even has Snake forge letters supposed to be between Lady Teazle and Charles. During the scenes in her house, she says less than Mrs Candour, though she often takes the lead in naming the target for malice. There is also a reference, easily missed by an audience, to her own suffering at the hands of scandalmongers: she has been 'Wounded myself in the early part of my life by the envenomed tongue of slander' (I.1.31–4). Despite this blight on her name, we learn that she is a widow, left 'with a good jointure' or fortune (I.1.49) and of course the social status of a title. Like the other members of the scandal school she fills her leisure with gossip and plotting 'mischief' (I.1.365).

Having established the theme of scandal in two significant early scenes with Lady Sneerwell, she disappears until Act V, where she appears briefly in the second scene, only to express her alarm at the suggestion of danger to Charles. Her final appearance, in the last scene, is again brief. Although her plot to compromise Charles and Lady Teazle by forged letters could have destroyed the happiness of the lovers, it is hard to take her seriously at this point; indeed, Sir Peter is amused when she appears, remarking: 'So another French milliner!' (V.3.163), indicating that he has recovered enough both to joke about the hiding of his wife behind the screen and to mock Lady Sneerwell. Snake's betrayal of her follows immediately and all Lady Sneerwell can do is utter her ineffectual curse (V.3.191–2) before retreating, dismissed as powerless by Sir Peter with the words: 'Oons, what a Fury!' (V.3.193).

JOSEPH SURFACE

Joseph is one of *The School for Scandal*'s most distinctive creations. He is established as a hypocrite from the very start, when Lady Sneerwell calls him 'artful, selfish, and malicious' and 'a sentimental knave' before he has even appeared on stage (I.1.72–3). Sheridan creates more than a mere stock villain in Joseph, however, and that is the reason why he has such appeal for an audience. He certainly caught the interest of contemporary commentators, and his name was being used as a shorthand term to insult Sheridan many years later.

Sheridan gives Joseph an extremely apt title: 'Mr Surface' is superficially moral but actually without any principles. He is also not 'an absolute Joseph' (IV.3.233) since unlike his biblical namesake

CONTEXT

A reviewer in the *Morning Chronicle* of 24 May 1777, felt that Joseph should have been given greater prominence: 'The character of Joseph might, and indeed ought to have been amplified; the first two acts ... might then have been spared; and the comedy would have deserved the title of the Man of Sentiment, a title much more expressive than it bears, and which, strictly speaking, is a gross misnomer.'

he is quite happy to corrupt others (see **Extended commentaries – Text 3**); his only interest in Maria is 'her fortune' (I.1.58) and he is prepared to seduce his friend Sir Peter's wife whilst apparently pursuing Maria. This 'avarice of crimes' angers Lady Sneerwell and he himself confesses, in a fine example of his true morality (that is, immorality), that he 'deviated from the direct road of wrong' by not being single-minded in his villainy (V.3.19, 21–2).

Lady Sneerwell knows Joseph's true nature and it is clear that other characters are also aware of his duplicity. Charles implies he has seen Lady Teazle alone at Joseph's house on earlier occasions and the servant knows where she 'always leaves her chair' when she calls (IV.3.11). Sir Oliver is contemptuous of his 'morality' even before he has met him (II.3.63) – it seems only Sir Peter cannot see through him. Sheridan makes his hypocrisy quite clear, in other words – but he also makes it interesting. He gives Joseph a distinctively sententious way of speaking, a pattern that soon becomes familiar to the audience, from his first 'moral sentiment' about 'the man who does not share in the distresses of a brother ...' (I.1.106–7) to the superbly **ironic** condemnation of his own conduct when, with Sir Peter's wife concealed behind the screen, he decries: 'the man who can break the laws of hospitality and attempt the wife of his friend' (IV.3.173–5). Sheridan is able to use this mannerism to comic effect when Rowley teases Sir Peter with an imitation of Joseph at the end of the play: 'Nay, Sir Peter, he who once lays aside suspicion – ' (V.2.248). It is a clear sign of Sir Peter's changed character that he so robustly declares in response: 'never let me hear you utter anything like a sentiment' (V.2.249–50).

CONTEXT

Jack Palmer, who first played Joseph, was clearly well suited to the part: James Boaden later recalled that he 'had a sort of elaborate grace and stately superiority, which he affected on all occasions' (from Boaden's biography of John Philip Kemble (1825), cited in Loftis, *Sheridan and the Drama of Georgian England*, p. 101).

Joseph tells the audience in **soliloquy** that he knows full well he is offering 'sentimental French plate' (V.1.102–8) when he talks in his moralistic way, and he enjoys the fact that it costs him nothing. Charles Lamb, writing in 1822 about his fond memories of the first production of *The School for Scandal*, identified this self-conscious acting of his hypocritical role as the reason for Jack Palmer's success: 'I remember the gay boldness, the graceful solemn plausibility, the measured step, the insinuating voice – to express it in a word – the downright *acted* villainy of the part, so different from the pressure of conscious actual wickedness – the hypocritical assumption of hypocrisy, – which made Jack so deservedly a favourite in that character ...' (Charles Lamb writing in the *London Magazine* of 1812, cited in Davidson (ed.), *Sheridan: Comedies*, p. 138). As an audience we should realise that Joseph is playing a part, and for most of the play, relishing it – this is made obvious when Lady Sneerwell ticks him off for trotting out a 'moral' in private (see I.1.109–11). Joseph's 'morals' are not high principles of behaviour (he dismisses Lady Teazle's reference to '*honour*' as 'the ill effects of your country education' which now stand in the way of her committing adultery, IV.3.89), but merely fine-sounding 'sentiments' that he does not believe in himself.

Joseph Surface is a suitable partner in crime for Lady Sneerwell, as Sir Oliver comments: Joseph is the 'oil' to her 'vinegar' (V.3.204), referring to the way that his smooth, duplicitous tones complement her acid wit – together they make a perfectly scandalous couple. Unlike with Charles, there is no reformation in Joseph's character suggested by Sheridan; Joseph leaves the stage for the last time still pretending to protect the brother he has been seeking to cheat throughout the play. Sir Peter, now cured of his own love of moralising, mockingly remarks that Joseph's undiminished hypocrisy makes him 'Moral to the last drop!' (V.3.203).

CHARLES SURFACE

Charles is portrayed by Sheridan as a genuine contrast to his brother Joseph, but is by no means a saint. Although in a comedy of this kind the outcome is never seriously in doubt, Sheridan needs to suggest some uncertainty along the way and in the case of Charles he does so by making him not merely a younger son who is the victim of his older brother's greed (including greed for Maria, the love of his life) but also by portraying him as a drinker and spendthrift who has no respect for his family possessions and traditions. He has therefore lost the respect of Sir Peter and comes close to losing the support of Sir Oliver, who had initially instinctively taken his side. His innate generosity, however, twice saves him when he is visited by Sir Oliver in disguise. He not only shows affection for Sir Oliver's portrait but also offers practical help for his poor relation Stanley when he can ill-afford the money.

CONTEXT

The essayist William Hazlitt (1778–1830) was also full of praise for the acting of Jack Palmer. 'With what an air he trod the stage! – With what pomp he handed Lady Teazle to a chair! With what elaborate duplicity he knelt to Maria!' (review in the *Examiner* of 1815, cited in Davidson (ed.), *Sheridan: Comedies*, pp. 136–7).

Although Charles is the successful suitor of Maria and the victor in the test of virtue that Sir Oliver devises to determine the heir to his fortune, Sheridan does not treat him as the conventional hero. Compared to his antagonist Joseph his role is comparatively small – he does not appear on stage until Act III – and there is no romantic scene with Maria (they only appear on stage together for a short time in the last scene). Charles, however, wins the audience's support through the good humour and high spirits he shows throughout. As Rowley says, 'There's no making you serious a moment' (IV.1.155). Unlike his brother he is direct and honest (Sheridan's drafts show that at one stage he even planned to give him the name Frank): 'the plain state of the matter is this: I am an extravagant young fellow who want money to borrow,' he declares, adding, 'Plain dealing in business I always think best' (III.3.114–16, 124). Without realising he is being tested by Joseph and the eavesdropping Sir Peter, he says, 'I hope I shall never deliberately do a dishonourable action' (IV.3.281–2) and it is clear that Sheridan expects the audience, as well as Sir Peter, to believe him. Sheridan rewards Charles with his young bride at the end of the play, and we are asked to accept his reformation without the need for promises, for '[Maria] shall be my monitor, my gentle guide. Ah! Can I leave the virtuous path those eyes illumine?' (V.3.244–6). This trust in the reforming power of love could be seen as an example of Sheridan's concession to the contemporary taste for a sentimental ending.

QUESTION

How attractive do you find Sheridan's portrayal of Charles? Do you find his 'reform' at the end of the play convincing?

Sheridan's characterisation of Charles differs from the outspoken reprobate heroes in the Restoration comedies of manners that he admired. Unlike Mirabell in Congreve's *The Way of the World* (1700), Charles does not win his love by the brilliance of his wit but by the essential generosity of his character. In his defence of pleasure-seeking Sheridan does allow him a sardonic sense of humour: describing his gambling and drinking habits, he says, 'I am now never so successful as when I am a little merry. Let me throw on a bottle of champagne, and I never lose – at least never feel my losses, which is exactly the same thing' (III.3.17–19). In this, he might seem to resemble some of Oscar Wilde's creations, Wilde being English theatre's next successful writer of comedies of manners. Lord Illingworth in *A Woman of No Importance* (1893) is similarly devoted to extravagant living but Wilde deliberately leaves him without the innate goodness that Charles possesses – like Joseph, Illingworth's charms are superficial despite his intelligence and good breeding. In that respect, Charles more closely resembles Wilde's younger hero, Gerald, from the same play, who wins the hand of a wealthy and principled heiress (Hester) because of his virtues and despite his lack of wit and social status.

SIR OLIVER SURFACE

Sir Oliver is portrayed by Sheridan as a reliable judge of character and events, whose wisdom (and wealth) will bring about a satisfactory conclusion to the play. Sheridan also sets up the situation so that he is both conveniently rich from his time in India and has been absent for fifteen years. This enables him to visit the brothers in disguise and provides a final comic moment when they both try to bundle him off the stage in the final scene, though they each mistake him for a different person. His pleasure in acting the part of a broker also allows Sheridan to introduce some **satire** at the expense of moneylenders.

Sir Oliver is indulgent of the excesses of the younger brother before he has even met him, and rather easily swayed when he does, going from saying, 'I'll never forgive him' (III.3.223), to 'I forgive him everything!' (IV.1.104) when his nephew shows affection for his portrait. However, unlike his friend Sir Peter, he bases his judgements on observing the brothers in action and he is never deceived in the way Sir Peter is. He takes against Joseph's sentiments as soon as hears of them: 'If he salutes me with a scrap of morality in his mouth, I shall be sick directly' (II.3.62–3), a reaction the audience surely shares. His final decision in favour of Charles, although it is governed to a certain extent by his own prejudices, also meets with the approval of the audience.

QUESTION
What is the importance of Sir Oliver in the play? Is he merely a plot device to test the two brothers, or does he have a wider role?

ROWLEY

Sheridan links Rowley more with Sir Oliver than with his master Sir Peter, for like Sir Oliver, Rowley has the ability to discern true merit. He is a trusted servant, or retainer, of many years' standing who had been steward to Joseph and Charles' father. As both he and Sir Peter are of an older generation, they adopt a respectful tone of address for each other, with Sir Peter calling him 'Master Rowley' (I.2.19) – a contrast, for example, with the over-familiarity of Trip, and Joseph's general ill-temper with his servant, who is only named when his master is putting on an appearance for Rowley (V.1.116). Rowley is the voice of good sense; he informs us at this first appearance that Sir Peter really loves Lady Teazle (I.2.26) and puts in a good word on behalf of Charles from the start, when everyone else appears to be against him. By linking his support of Charles to an implied criticism of Joseph ('I only wish you may not be deceived in your opinion of the elder [brother]', I.2.41–2), whose hypocrisy we have already seen, Sheridan ensures we are favourably inclined to both Rowley and Charles – and at the end, Sir Peter recognises this by referring to him as 'honest Rowley' (V.2.220). Rowley is also used to advance the plot: he brings news of Sir Oliver's arrival, fetches Moses to Sir Oliver to set up the visit to Charles' house, arranges for Snake to be bribed to tell the truth and is on hand for the **denouement** in Act V. Although a minor character, Sheridan allows Rowley to develop a little, giving him a joke at Sir Peter's expense at the end of Act V Scene 2, when he mimics one of Joseph's sentiments and provokes Sir Peter to declare that he is quite cured of his illusions (V.2.248–11).

WWW. CHECK THE NET

The actors in early productions would have worn clothes of their own time. You can find illustrations of late eighteenth century costumes on the The Costumer's Manifesto website, **www.costumes.org**. Find the link to '(Costume) History sorted by Period' and follow links to the 1770s. As well as men's and women's fashions the site has illustrations of some of the fanciful ladies' wigs that Charles mocks in IV.1.49.

MARIA

Maria, the young ward of Sir Peter, is central to the romantic plot of *The School for Scandal.* She is the one whom Charles loves, though his brother seeks to marry her for her money and Sir Benjamin also claims to be in love with her. To make matters worse for her, her guardian has forbidden her to see Charles and would compel her to marry Joseph – and Lady Sneerwell attempts by gossip and forged letters to prove that Charles is in love with Lady Teazle. She is, however, not given a major role by Sheridan, perhaps because he was forced to use an inexperienced actor for the part (see **Detailed summary** for **Act V Scene 3**) or perhaps because he did not wish to detract from the central female role he had given to Lady Teazle. Maria's name signifies that, like Charles, she is not a 'type' (though there may be an implied link to the Virgin Mary to suggest her purity in contrast to the corruption that surrounds her). She stands out from the scandal school, indicating by her distress that their gossip, whilst witty, can also be harmful – and also taking a clear stand against scandal. Her comment to Mrs Candour, ''Tis strangely impertinent for people to busy themselves so' (I.1.186), is just one of her critical observations throughout the scenes with the scandal school.

Although Maria is regularly referred to by other characters as 'child', Sheridan does give her an independent spirit. She resists Sir Peter's attempts to make her respond to Joseph and even when, in the final scene, it appears the way is clear for her to marry Charles she will not do so whilst there is the suggestion that he loves Lady Sneerwell. In the end, true feeling wins and she is united with Charles, though without the audience hearing her actually agree to his proposal (V.3.231).

QUESTION

What does Maria's silence at the end of the play (V.3.224–33) say about her character and/or the role of women at the time?

THE SCANDAL SCHOOL

The members of Lady Sneerwell's school are comic types created to demonstrate the vacuous life led by this section of society, for whom malicious gossip is a diversion. The inclusion of two men in this group is perhaps a suggestion by Sheridan that scandalmongering is not an exclusively female preoccupation – though we notice that Maria describes a man who spreads scandal as particularly 'contemptible' (I.1.158).

QUESTION

How far would you agree with Joseph's claim that the scandalmongers 'have no malice at heart' (II.2.190–1)?

Mrs Candour is a particularly dubious character, as indicated by her name. By Sheridan's time, 'candour' had acquired the additional, **ironic** meaning of disguising malice as frankness, as demonstrated by everything Mrs Candour says. She certainly says a great deal, despite her protests that 'I never will join in ridiculing a friend' (II.2.117). In her final appearance, in Act V Scene 2, she reminds us how important scandal is to her, fearing she will not be able to spread the news of the misfortune suffered by her 'friends' before it is in the newspapers. However, by this stage she can do no real harm, since Sir Peter has come to his senses and no longer fears for the fidelity of his wife – he merely drives her and the others out of his house. Sheridan differentiates her pretended concern for the objects of her gossip from the more openly malicious gossip of the two men in the group.

CONTEXT

Mr Dodd, who played the first Sir Benjamin, was described as 'the prince of pink heels, and the soul of empty eminence' (James Boaden, *Memoirs of the Life of John Philip Kemble*, 1825, Volume 1, p. 55).

CONTEXT

Italian in origin, the term 'macaronis' refers specifically to the upper class men who went on Grand Tours of Europe and acquired foreign tastes. Horace Walpole wrote to a friend in 1764 about 'the Macaroni Club, which is composed of all the travelled young men who wear long curls and spying-glasses' (Paget Toynbee (ed.), *The Letters of Horace Walpole*, 1904, Volume 5, pp. 449–50).

Sir Benjamin Backbite's character is also summed up in his name. As he says: 'my little productions are mostly satires and lampoons on particular people', which he prefers to 'circulate' behind people's backs than to publish in the papers – ''tis very vulgar to print' (I.1.254–6). Although he refers to his 'love elegies' to Maria (I.1.258) it is surely impossible to take him seriously as her lover. He seems to pay almost no attention to her on stage for he is portrayed by Sheridan as more interested in gossiping and talking about himself. He is particularly concerned about the appearance of his poetry on the page ('a neat rivulet of text shall meander through a meadow of margin', I.1.264–5) and his poetry, when we hear it in II.2.11–14, is typically foolish. He could be described himself, like the ponies in his verse, as a 'macaroni' – an affected fop. His final appearance in Act V Scene 2 is if anything even more satirical, concerned as he is to outdo everyone in his sensational account of the fictitious duel.

Crabtree, Sir Benjamin's uncle, is an appropriate foil, with his exaggerated praise for his nephew, whom he ridiculously compares to the famous Italian poet Petrarch (I.1.261). However, he too is more interested in gossip: 'Have you heard the news?' (I.1.267). He and his nephew operate as a double act; the scandal in the first scene alternates between them, each adding a further morsel of gossip about Charles, for example (I.1.315–32), and continuing even after it is obvious that they have upset Maria, with whom Sir Benjamin is supposed to be in love. This scene ends with the two of them, on the point of leaving, each comically returning several times to complete 'a subject they have not quite run down' (I.1.358–9).

SNAKE

The 'precious rogue' Snake makes his role clear in the final scene: 'I live by the badness of my character. I have nothing but my infamy to depend on' (V.3.215–16, 221). Theatrical tradition has Snake dressed in black, perhaps suggesting the clergyman on whom it was believed Sheridan based his character (see **Extended Commentaries – Text 1**). Black certainly suits his occupation as a spreader of rumour and destroyer of reputations. As Joseph says of him: 'that fellow hasn't virtue enough to be faithful even to his own villainy' (I.1.127–9). His function in the plot, apart from being used in the opening lines to draw an explanation from Lady Sneerwell of her attitudes to the Surface brothers, is to be paid by Rowley at the end of the play to betray the plots she and Joseph have concocted. It is in this final scene that Sheridan transforms Snake from a mere plot device into a more interesting character. With nice **irony** Snake begs that his good deed remain secret as his livelihood depends on his 'infamy'. Unlike Joseph, Snake has no desire for a good reputation – suggesting the real values underlying the society of the time.

WWW. CHECK THE NET

Wikipedia has a page on macaronis, which includes some caricatures from 1773 and 1774. Go to the homepage **www.en.wikipedia.org** and type 'macaroni (fashion)' into the search box.

TRIP

Trip appears only briefly in two scenes at Charles' house. Sheridan creates a vivid caricature of an extravagant servant who affects his master's ways. He takes snuff like a gentleman and has also adopted society affectations by wearing an ornament in his hair and buying bouquets of flowers – as a result he, like his master, is in debt and wants to borrow money. Even the lower classes, Sheridan seems to say, have been corrupted by the immorality of London society.

MOSES

Moses, like Snake and Trip, has a minor part in the plot but here too Sheridan conveys some of the attitudes of his time. Moses, as a Jew, is an outsider given a stereotypical role as moneylender, with traces of a foreign accent ('want the moneys very bad', III.1.94–5). He is treated sympathetically, however; Charles calls him 'honest Moses' and seems to mean it (III.3.79), and he is in fact not the moneylender himself but the broker attempting to help Charles raise money from a Christian lender. (For the possibility that this is a subtle reference to the prominent banker Benjamin Hopkins see the **Detailed summary** for **Act III Scene 1**.) Sheridan also uses his conversations with Sir Oliver and Charles to **satirise** both moneylenders and those whose extravagance is such that they do not care about the exorbitant rates of interest charged by them.

CONTEXT

'Honest Israelite' (III.1.44) is an echo of Jesus' words in the New Testament: 'Behold an Israelite indeed, in whom is no guile!' (John 1:47).

CONTEXT

In the late eighteenth century, scandal was a term used to describe the circulation of shocking stories about members of the middle and upper classes, usually in the newspapers.

CONTEXT

Many in Sheridan's audience would have recognised in the invented tales in Act V Scene 2 a reference to Sheridan's two duels with Thomas Mathews in 1772. 'The ridiculous and contradictory reports then afloat, certainly gave rise to the highly humorous duel scenes in *The Rivals* and *The School for Scandal,'* Sheridan's niece Alicia Lefanu later wrote (cited in Loftis, *Sheridan and the Drama of Georgian England*, p. 44).

THEMES

SCANDAL AND REPUTATION

Teach me, pow'rful Genius! teach
  Thine own mysterious art,
Safe from Retaliation's reach,
  How I may throw Detraction's dart!

Sheridan, *Ode to the Genius of Scandal* (1781)

Scandalmongering was not, of course, new in Sheridan's time, nor was he the first to **satirise** it. It had however found an effective new market with the recent launch of the *Town and Country Magazine* and the *Morning Post*, with their gossip columns full of thinly disguised references to members of London's fashionable society. Snake refers to these publications in the opening lines, and Garrick's Prologue has Mr King (Sir Peter) reading snippets from the gossip columns. In beginning his play with the reference to the 'paragraphs' (I.1.1), Sheridan harnesses a topical feature that would be familiar to his London audience. It also had personal significance for the playwright as a vivid memory from his own courtship and elopement with Eliza. His rival Mathews had posted a notice in the *Bath Chronicle* about 'Mr Richard S', saying 'I cannot longer think he deserves the treatment of a gentleman, than in this public method to post him as a L., and a treacherous S.' By calling Sheridan a 'liar' and a 'scoundrel', Mathews ensured that Sheridan either had to respond by fighting a duel or accept a grave insult to his reputation.

The effects of scandal in *The School for Scandal* are less dramatic, however, and Sheridan's account is more a satire at the expense of the specific scandal school he invents. The objects of their slander, with comic names such as Miss Gadabout, Sir Filigree Flirt, Widow Ochre and Miss Sallow, mean nothing to the audience and we are no more concerned about their feelings than are Mrs Candour or Sir Benjamin Backbite. The subjects of their gossip are often familiar today: love affairs, marriage, pregnancy and divorce. There are also other concerns, more specific to the late eighteenth century: duels, bankruptcy and relationships across social boundaries ('Miss Nicely is going to be married to her own footman!', I.1.269–70). Sheridan keeps the audience's interest by varying the objects and forms of the scandal. The play opens with a discussion between Snake and Lady Sneerwell of scandal as an art, in which she is praised for her ability to 'do more with a word or a look than many can with the most laboured detail' (I.1.26–8). They organise notices in the papers, forged letters and rumours, while later Sir Benjamin recites his ridiculous poem mocking two ponies and Mrs Candour provides us with plenty of 'laboured detail' at the expense of her friends and relations. All this is conveyed with such wit that the audience might agree with Joseph that 'conversation where the spirit of raillery is suppressed will ever appear tedious and insipid' (I.1.155–6). The final appearance of the scandal school, each member vying to outdo the other with more sensational accounts of the fictitious duel in Act V Scene 2, is made ridiculous by Sheridan with the absurd nature of their inventions (see especially, V.2.88–90). Although Sir Peter drives them out, Sheridan implies that they are undeterred and that scandal will continue unabated: 'depend on't, we'll make the best report of it we can,' is Mrs Candour's parting shot (V.2.157–8). The difference is that now, as Rowley says, Sir Peter no longer worries about what they may say: 'Without affectation, Sir Peter, you may despise the ridicule of fools' (V.2.216–17).

There are however moments when the potential consequences of scandal are taken more seriously. Lady Sneerwell refers in the opening lines to 'the envenomed tongue of slander' that has caused her 'own injured reputation' (I.1.32–4), which explains her malice towards others. Sir Peter claims to despise rumour yet he takes Joseph's public reputation at face value ('Everybody in the world speaks well of him', II.3.52) and he is clearly distressed by the stories circulating about Lady Teazle and Charles, indicating that he both listens to rumour and gives it some credit. Maria, though her own reputation is untouched by scandal, is distressed by the 'perpetual libel' of Sir Benjamin's conversation (I.1.141) and even more by the delight the scandalmongers take in Charles' financial distress. In the final scene, Maria reveals that she has been taken in by the rumours about Charles – in convincing her that Charles and

CHECK THE BOOK

Jane Austen's readers clearly understood society's moral framework; in *Mansfield Park* (1814), it is feared that Mrs Rushworth has committed an 'at least very flagrant indiscretion'; when it becomes known that she has run away with Henry Crawford, 'all was lost on the side of character' (Chapter 47).

> **QUESTION**
> How seriously is scandal ridiculed in the play? Is it easy to draw a line between the moral tones of *The School for Scandal* and the enjoyment we are encouraged to derive from its florid displays of wit and malice?

Lady Sneerwell are lovers, scandal still threatens Maria's happiness even after the **denouement** of the play.

Lady Teazle's discovery is the most dramatic, however. Act IV Scene 3 begins with Sheridan gently mocking her annoyance that others are again talking about her: 'And there's my friend Lady Sneerwell has circulated I don't know how many scandalous tales of me, and all without any foundation too. That's what vexes me' (IV.3.33–5). At this stage it still seems a game to Lady Teazle, and one which Joseph is anxious to continue by encouraging her to give herself to him, to make the rumours true. However, with the arrival of Sir Peter the truth dawns: 'I'm ruined!' she cries (IV.3.99). Sheridan's poem, *Ode to the Genius of Scandal*, depicts a 'weeping maid' ruined by rumour, a reflection of a reality the audience would have recognised. For any society woman of the period except the most wealthy, appearance and reputation were her most precious assets. The objects of the scandal school's attacks are almost all women; whilst it amuses Sir Peter when he thinks Joseph has a 'French milliner' behind the screen, it would have ruined Lady Teazle to have been known as Joseph's lover. As this is a comedy, however, Sheridan brings about a happy resolution in which reputation is preserved – though to the audience it is clear that scandal is only averted, not completely crushed.

Whilst Lady Sneerwell, Snake and Joseph use subterfuge to destroy reputations, Sir Oliver and Rowley also resort to deception in order to uncover the truth. By calling Joseph 'Surface', Sheridan indicates the superficiality of his reputation, but he also demonstrates this clearly in Joseph's actions – both in his dealings with women and in his behaviour towards Sir Oliver when he believes he is a poor relation, Mr Stanley. Joseph tells the audience that 'there needs no small degree of address to gain the reputation of benevolence without incurring the expense' (V.1.103–5). His brother, meanwhile, redeems his reputation in Sir Oliver's eyes by demonstrating real compassion, first for his uncle's portrait and then for Stanley. In the 'screen scene', Sheridan completes his vindication of Charles by rejecting any suggestion that he was interested in Lady Teazle. He does this with characteristic **dramatic**

irony: Charles says to Joseph, 'Well, I believe I should be obliged to borrow a little of your morality' (IV.3.286–7), reminding us again that Joseph's reputation is all on the surface. A reflective audience member might notice, as Victorian commentators certainly did, that Charles' reputation as a rake and spendthrift seems thoroughly deserved and yet, whilst nominally condemned, it is overlooked in the light of the virtues he demonstrates towards the end of the play.

However, that may be taking too literal an approach to a play, which is, after all, a comedy. Sheridan's **satire** is focused on the gossip of the scandalmongers and the hypocrisy of Joseph; as part of the more **sentimental** tone of the ending the audience is asked to accept that Charles will indeed be reformed by the power of Maria's virtue.

MONEY AND MARRIAGE

Sheridan was writing in a time of increasing wealth, at least for the middle and upper classes. This was partly a result of an expanding empire – Sir Oliver has made his fortune in 'the East Indies' – and partly through growth in trade and industry. Lady Sneerwell is 'the widow of a City knight' (I.1.48–9) – that is a London merchant, a member of a newer aristocracy than the landed gentry. The reality of poverty was not far away, however, especially for someone like Sheridan with no inherited wealth and who knew that the family home and possessions in Ireland had been auctioned off when he was eight. Sheridan was constantly borrowing money, whether to invest in a share of the Theatre Royal Drury Lane or to maintain the kind of life he needed to mix with fashionable society. Debt – as he himself was to experience many years later – could result in being confined to a 'sponging house' or debtors' prison, like poor Stanley in the play.

The original audience would have been well acquainted with the importance of a good financial settlement as the basis for a marriage. In his previous success, *The Rivals*, Sheridan had mocked the heroine's romantic desire for an impoverished lover – and transformed him into the heir of a wealthy knight at the end of the

CONTEXT

Sheridan owed £2,000 to a moneylender called Jacob Nathan Moses – probably a debt he took over from Willoughby Lacy when he bought his share of the Drury Lane Theatre. As Fintan O'Toole comments, the situation reminds us of *The School for Scandal*: 'Lacy's situation as a decent young man in debt to a moneylender may have provided Sheridan with the idea of having Charles Surface in debt to a moneylender called Moses' (*A Traitor's Kiss*, p. 128).

play. In *The School for Scandal*, Maria is sought by Joseph purely because of 'her fortune' (I.1.58) and she cannot marry Charles whilst he has no money – in any case, she is still under the control of her guardian, Sir Peter. Once Charles has proved his virtues sufficiently to satisfy Sir Oliver that the younger son shall be his heir, his wealth is assured and Sir Peter is happy to agree to a marriage the very next day, even though, as Maria protests, she has herself said nothing in agreement (V.3.230–1). Sir Peter is of course characterised by Sheridan as being in many ways a typical tyrannical guardian, as obstinate in his opposition to the young lovers as he is in his attitudes to his wife. As Sheridan knew from the opposition he faced to his own marriage to Elizabeth Linley, this would not seem completely unrealistic to an audience; he himself was forbidden by his father from even communicating with Elizabeth for some months after they had returned from France where they had gone through a nominal marriage ceremony.

QUESTION

Today marriage and money are no longer so absolutely linked as they were in the eighteenth century. This is just one example of how social values have changed since the time of the play. What other examples can you find?

Sir Peter's relationship with Lady Teazle is the other portrait of marriage in the play. Sheridan creates a stock comic situation with a 'pretty woman married to a man old enough to be her father,' as Charles says (IV.3.283–4). The account of their courtship in Act III Scene 1 reinforces this image; it is clear from her approaches to him for money, and the subsequent arguments about her extravagance, that Sheridan wants us to believe that the prospect of a comfortable London life was her main attraction to Sir Peter. 'What, though I was educated in the country, I know very well that women of fashion in London are accountable to nobody after they are married,' is how Sheridan describes Lady Teazle's attitude (II.1.4–6). The reality is rather different – after all, she still has to ask him for money – and by the end of the play we are invited to believe that the couple have each seen the error of their expectations and 'intend' to live 'happily' (V.3.234–5). This could be seen as Sheridan's concession to **sentimental comedy**, though Sir Peter's use of the word 'intend' indicates some comic **ambiguity** and Lady Teazle's Epilogue (written by Colman), describing her return to dull country pursuits, also has an **ironic** feel.

If money was important in eighteenth-century marriage, it was also essential for a place in society. Sheridan uses Charles' desire for money in order to live the life of a young society buck, drinking, gambling and enjoying himself, as an opportunity for some **satire** at the expense of moneylenders and those who borrow from them. Resorting to a type familiar from Shakespeare's Shylock in *The Merchant of Venice*, his moneylender appears to be a Jew, though Sheridan subverts expectations by telling us that Moses is no longer willing or able to risk any more money on Charles and is instead acting as a broker for a Christian lender. He still expects his commission, however: when Charles works out how much he has gained by the sale of the pictures in Act IV Scene 1, the audience would be expected to know that a third of the £800 goes to Moses. Charles also jests with 'Mr Premium' about the exorbitant rates of interest, but admits his desire for money is such that he is 'blockhead enough to give fifty percent sooner than not have it, and you ... are rogue enough to take a hundred if you can get it' (III.3.117–19). Sheridan also includes topical references to the Annuity Bill, then going through Parliament, which was intended to protect under-age borrowers (of which Charles may be one). Sheridan thus targets both unscrupulous lenders and irresponsible borrowers in the play, though the resolution depends on the appearance of more unearned wealth for Charles from his 'dev'lish rich uncle in the East Indies, Sir Oliver Surface' (III.3.146–7) – and, of course, on the money Maria has inherited from her late father.

CONTEXT

The Annuity Bill (mentioned by Sir Peter in II.1.110) was being debated in Parliament at the time the play was first performed (it become law later that month). It required annuities to be registered, limited interest rates, and outlawed contracts with minors (those under twenty-one).

MORALITY

It might seem odd to consider *The School for Scandal* as a moral play when an audience is most likely to recall the witty dialogue and comic scenes. Garrick's Prologue implies as much: 'Cut Scandal's head off, still the tongue is wagging' (Prologue, line 34). Satire as a dramatic convention suggests however that weakness, folly or vice will be exposed and this does occur by the end of the play; even though we may accept that tongues will still wag, wiser heads may, Sheridan implies, have learnt to dismiss what they say. It is also possible to detect an underlying morality, which indicates the influence of sentimental comedy as well as reflecting the standards of Sheridan's own time. Although Charles may live a dissolute life for a while, he will need to reform once he marries Maria. Even if his words are jocular, he does pledge himself to virtue under her

CONTEXT

At the time of Sheridan's death in 1816 an article in the *Gentleman's Magazine* lamented that he 'did not apply himself with more care to improve the heart and stimulate the public mind to the cultivation of morality.'

guidance: 'Can I leave the virtuous path those eyes illumine?' (V.3.245–6). It is perhaps significant that Maria is the example of moral virtue; whilst other women may gossip, she alone is untouched by the temptation to spread scandal or indulge in scandalous behaviour. She asserts her independence against her guardian in Act III Scene 1, but accepts his authority over her as a dutiful ward should. Even when the path to marriage with Charles seems clear, she will not take him whilst there is a suggestion of a relationship with another woman. Virtue, it is implied, is a particularly female characteristic just as the loss of reputation was a disaster for women at that time.

Maria's livelier counterpart is Lady Teazle. Sheridan shows her succumbing to the temptations of fashionable society by learning to spread scandal and even taking a lover, though 'no farther than fashion requires' (II.2.228). The playwright deliberately maintains Lady Teazle's distance from the scandalmongers, however, in order that he can at the end effect her reversion to traditional morality. Whilst Lady Teazle is genuinely tempted by Joseph, she does not indulge in Joseph's sophistry about the seduction and realises that she is be about to 'do wrong' (IV.3.92) – she still has enough of her 'country prejudices' left to see this (II.2.231). Hearing Sir Peter talk of his regard for her from behind the screen causes her heart to respond, so that she speaks in moral terms, using the phrases 'honour', 'shame' and 'the sincerity of my gratitude' (IV.3.403, 411–13). We are to believe that at the end of the play she and her husband will live happily, away from the evils of London's corrupt society, where, as Jean-Jacques Rousseau put it, 'each [man] easily hiding his conduct from the public eye, shows himself only by his reputation' ('Letter to M. D'Alembert', cited in O'Toole, *A Traitor's Kiss*, p. 122). Sheridan had enough experience of fashionable society in both Bath and London to know that love affairs and sexual liaisons (though no doubt as common as the gossip in the opening scene implies) were to be discreet. There is a glimpse of the double standards that governed sexual mores at the time when Charles accuses Joseph of having 'a Jew or a wench' with him (IV.3.253–6). Both Sir Peter and Charles seem more amused than shocked that Joseph might have a 'French milliner' in his house. As with the different rules that existed for men and for women in matters of the heart, with a higher value placed on a lady's reputation, men were also far freer to keep mistresses from the lower orders without risk to their social standing than they were to dally with upper or middle class ladies. Like debt, however, the real details of any affairs had to be kept secret.

Sir Peter and Sir Oliver also represent moral standards at odds with those of fashionable society. Whilst Sir Peter needs to learn the error of his obstinacy and self-deception, he is never tempted to gossip. Sir Oliver acts as a kindly judge, who resorts to deception only to uncover what is in the hearts of his two nephews. He recognises, as the audience is invited to agree, that not only is Joseph a hypocrite but Charles is genuinely compassionate despite his dissolute lifestyle. Sheridan seems careful to show Charles indulging only in extravagance – wine, gambling and living beyond his means – rather than moral depravity. While Joseph has only 'sentimental French plate' (V.1.107) and will not part with a penny to help Stanley, Charles' good nature is demonstrated by his open generosity to his poor relation, which Sheridan implies cancels out his failings. Indeed, Sir Oliver, and perhaps Sir Peter too, themselves stand as examples of extravagance reformed – in his youth Sir Oliver joined his brother, the boys' father, in the kind of high-spirited but essentially harmless behaviour Charles displays. This serves to align Charles' minor dissolution with the older, more respectable generation, while Joseph's alienation from family and fortune could not be more complete.

THE ROLE OF WOMEN

To woman ev'ry charm was giv'n,
Design'd by all indulgent heav'n
    To soften ev'ry care.
Yes! ye were form'd to bless mankind,
To harmonize and soothe the mind,
    Indeed, indeed ye were!

Sheridan, *Ode to the Genius of Scandal* (1781)

Sheridan's female characters reflect the social conditions of his day. He created a range of brilliantly characterised roles for his female actors, from the incessantly gossipy Mrs Candour to the

CONTEXT

Literature in the eighteenth century often referred to the dangers and temptations facing women, in particular the consequences of a real or supposed lapse in sexual morality. Samuel Richardson's (1689–1761) widely-read sentimental novel *Clarissa* (1747–8) centres on this theme. The heroine, taken in by 'the vows and oaths of a vile rake, whom she believes to be a man of honour' is abducted and then assaulted by him. As a result of this rape, she is 'persecuted by all her friends, and abandoned to the deepest distress' (Belford to Lovelace, Letter X, Volume 8).

magnificently witty Lady Teazle. Each is a character from her time. Despite Lady Teazle's boast to her husband, 'that women of fashion in London are accountable to nobody after they are married' (II.1.5–6), Sheridan does not challenge social conventions by allowing any of the women in his play to behave in a truly independent manner. If the malicious Lady Sneerwell has the freedom to act as she pleases, it is because she has been left a good fortune by her late husband – a reminder of women's financial dependence on men at the time – and we are aware that she seeks happiness by attempting to win, and presumably to marry, Charles. This is reinforced by Maria's need to conform to her guardian's wishes (despite the fact that she has been left a good inheritance) and Lady Teazle's requests to Sir Peter for more money – like Lady Sneerwell, it is made clear that Lady Teazle would only really be free once her husband is dead and she has access to his wealth. Part of the humour of Sir Peter's defeats at the hands of his wife in Act II Scene 1 and Act III Scene 1 is that this goes against the social norms, though the audience is also likely to feel he has deserved this treatment by ill-advisedly marrying a young wife.

CONTEXT

In addition to her popular romantic novel *Memoirs of Miss Sidney Biddulph*, Sheridan's mother also wrote a successful comedy, *The Discovery* (1763). Frances Sheridan's literary successes flew in the face of her father who regarded writing as 'perfectly superfluous' in female education and had tried to prevent her from learning to read. There are similarities between Sheridan's intractable grandfather and the character of Sir Anthony Absolute he created in *The Rivals*.

It will be apparent to modern audiences that different standards apply to the men and women in the play. Whilst Joseph is condemned as a hypocrite, he walks away without consequences other than losing the hope of marrying Maria. He is permitted a 'French milliner' in his library, but Lady Teazle is not allowed to cross the boundaries of sexual propriety. Charles leads a careless and selfish life – it is to his wife-to-be that he looks for guidance and moral purity at the end. It is true that Sheridan features both men and women in his scandal school, but their leader is a woman and their targets are mostly women, mocked for trying to hide their age or imperfections, or criticised for sexual indiscretions. Maria makes these double standards plain when she says to Joseph: 'We have pride, envy, rivalship, and a thousand motives to depreciate each other; but the male slanderer must have the cowardice of a woman before he can traduce [speak badly of] one' (I.1.158–61). Women may be excused for gossiping, it seems, more readily than men – Maria implies that this is because nothing better is expected of them, such is their assumed predisposition to petty rivalry and spite, while nobility and bravery is reserved for men. Maria's wry words reflect the cutting **ironies** of Sheridan's *Ode* – women are expected to be perfect, but when they miss the mark it is into the den of 'hydra Scandal' that they fall (Prologue, line 38). With women themselves as their harshest critics it is not surprising that once fallen few recovered.

DRAMATIC TECHNIQUES

SENTIMENTAL AND LAUGHING COMEDY

> Yet thus adorned with every graceful art
> To charm the fancy and yet reach the heart,
> Must we displace her? And instead advance
> The goddess of the woeful countenance,
> The sentimental muse!
>
> Sheridan's Prologue to *The Rivals* (1775)

Sheridan was writing at a time of changing values in literature as well as politics. There was an increasing taste for literature upholding traditional Christian virtues in which the central character triumphs over considerable odds. At its root lay a belief, later developed by the Romantics, in the essential goodness of humanity and the ability of even the worst characters to see the error of their ways and reform. Richardson's *Clarissa* (see **Themes: Morality**) was extremely influential in this regard and, encouraged by Richardson, Sheridan's mother Frances had written a very popular romantic novel of this kind, called *Memoirs of Miss Sidney Biddulph* (1761). James Boswell commented: 'What it teaches is impressed upon the mind by a series of as deep distress as can affect humanity, in the amiable and pious heroine who goes to her grave unrelieved, but resigned' (Boswell, *The Life of Samuel Johnson* (1791), cited by Kelly, *Richard Brinsley Sheridan: A Life*, p. 17).

Sheridan's fellow playwright Oliver Goldsmith, writing in the *Westminster Magazine* in January 1773, asked, 'Which deserves the preference? The Weeping Sentimental Comedy, so much in fashion at present, or the Laughing and even Low Comedy?' His response was clear: 'Comedy should excite our laughter by ridiculously

? QUESTION

Are there other themes to be found in the play? For example, does Sheridan have interesting things to say about the differences between youth and age?

CONTEXT

Oliver Goldsmith (c.1730–74) was, like Sheridan, born in Ireland. He is today best remembered for his novel *The Vicar of Wakefield* (1766) and the play *She Stoops to Conquer* (1773). In this last work, Goldsmith gently mocks both the older generation, with a wife who would ape London fashion and a husband who talks interminably of military campaigns, and a young man who is so nervous in the presence of the woman he loves that it is only when she 'stoops' by pretending to be a barmaid that he will pursue her.

exhibiting the Follies of the Lower Part of Mankind.' In '*Sentimental* Comedy,' Goldsmith complained, there was little humour: 'the virtues of Private Life are exhibited, rather than the Vices exposed ... In these Plays almost all the characters are good and exceedingly generous; they are lavish enough of their *Tin* Money on the stage, and though they want Humour, have abundance of Sentiment and Feeling' (*Essay on the Theatre*). This thinly-disguised contempt for shallow feelings finds an echo in Sheridan's portrayal of Joseph in *The School for Scandal.*

Sheridan responds to this taste for sentiment without succumbing to it: in his Prologue to *The Rivals* comedy is said both 'to charm the fancy and yet reach the heart' – genuine emotions and a happy ending are not ruled out. In this earlier comedy the aptly-named heroine, Lydia Languish, has a taste for **sentimental** novels such as *The Delicate Distress*, *The Tears of Sensibility*, *The Sentimental Journey* and *The Man of Feeling* (this last title echoing descriptions of Joseph Surface). In *The School for Scandal* the **satire** is more biting than in the earlier play, with hypocrisy as a particular focus for criticism. Joseph is all sham, 'artful, selfish, and malicious' (I.1.72) and much of the comedy derives from his brazen application of his art and from his unmasking. The use of the term 'sentimental French plate' to describe Joseph's thin coating of feeling (V.1.107) is perhaps a reference to the *comédie larmoyante*, or 'tearful comedy', that had become popular in France in the eighteenth century. It was part of a general movement towards more public demonstrations of feeling that found full expression in Romanticism but also continued to attract criticism when it led to sentimentality – the focus of Sheridan's mockery in *The Rivals* and Jane Austen's satire in *Northanger Abbey* of 1818. In *The School for Scandal*, sentimentality is kept in check; although we learn that Lady Teazle is in tears after the screen scene, this (and her reconciliation with Sir Peter) takes place off-stage, while the on-stage depiction of 'sentiments' is entirely satirical.

CHECK THE BOOK

The Man of Feeling was the title of a popular novel published in 1771 by Henry Mackenzie. Its hero, who is ruled by a benevolent heart, visits London only to fall into the hands of people who exploit his innocence (**ironically** similar to the way the play's 'man of feeling', Joseph, seeks to take advantage of Maria and Lady Teazle). It inaugurated a vogue for a new kind of hero, the sensitive male who was not ashamed to weep, often seen in novels published in the years that followed. Mackenzie, who was in reality a hard-headed person followed his first novel with *The Man of the World* in 1773, in which the hero is a villain and seducer.

The scandalmongers are attacked for their malice and folly through brilliantly written dialogue in which they condemn themselves out of their own mouths – Mrs Candour is only the most obvious example. More in the manner of comedies by satirists such as

Jonson and Congreve, these comic types are exposed at the end of the play but they are unchanged; even Joseph and Lady Sneerwell leave without serious punishment and, in a nice satiric touch, Snake begs Sir Peter and Sir Oliver to preserve his infamous reputation. Sheridan seems to be implying laughingly that we cannot expect to banish slander and hypocrisy, merely learn to see through them – and enjoy doing so.

Gentler comic forces are also at play. Whilst Sir Peter and Lady Teazle are both misguided and their clashes in the earlier scenes are magnificent set pieces in a long tradition of dramatic conflicts between husbands and wives, they come to their senses later. In an earlier comedy, such as Wycherley's *The Country Wife* of 1675, Sir Peter would probably have been cuckolded and the audience expected to enjoy his misery; here, Lady Teazle realises the dreadful consequences of adultery just in time and Sir Peter admits his blindness to the wiles of Joseph. Charles too is reformed; it turns out that he, not his brother, is the true 'man of sentiment' for he has a generous heart and reaches into his pocket to help a fellow human being in distress. It is true to the nature of comedy that this fellow human happens to be his disguised rich uncle whose own warm heart and ample purse bring about Charles' restoration to wealth and thereby to the hand of his true love. This romantic ending reflects the taste of the time for virtue to be rewarded, just as the earlier unmasking of Joseph conforms to comic and satirical traditions.

BURLESQUE AND SATIRE

Sheridan's comedies are part of a long tradition of **burlesque** – that is, comic imitation of a serious subject or literary form. This is most obvious in the scenes involving the scandal school, with their comic names reminding us that they are to be seen as 'types' rather than as representations of real people. With references to the gossip columns in the papers available on the streets of London, the audience would not have missed this satire of fashionable follies. Sheridan dramatises his attacks by resorting to exaggeration in the early scene with Mrs Candour, while the satire reaches its culmination in the wildly inventive accounts in Act V Scene 2 of a

CHECK THE BOOK

In *The Alchemist* (1610) Ben Jonson (1572–1637) satirises greed and hypocrisy as Face, Subtle and Dol Common cheat a succession of gullible visitors with the promise of wealth from the philosopher's stone. Congreve's *The Way of the World* (1700) portrays a world in which sexual liaisons are openly tolerated and wit is valued above morality.

CHECK THE BOOK

'And so, by way of a contrast between the scandalmongers and the men of good will, there is established the distinctive tone of the play, that balance between sentiment and satire typical of the Age of Johnson at its best' (Loftis, *Sheridan and the Drama of Georgian England*, p. 99).

CONTEXT

M. H. Abrams in *A Glossary of Literary Terms* (Wadsworth, third edition, 2004) writes that 'the burlesque may be written for the sheer fun of it; usually, however, it is a form of satire' and that is the case with *The School for Scandal*. Sheridan's *The Critic* (1779) is a burlesque on the absurdities of sentimental and historical dramas of his time as well as on the cruelties of some literary critics. Abrams also points out that the word is often now used, especially in America, to describe a variety show – a significant difference from eighteenth century usage.

duel that never took place. Joseph's hypocrisy is another subject for satire – and in the process Sheridan also burlesques the current uncritical taste for 'noble sentiments' (see **Sentimental and laughing comedy**).

While satire relies on characters that are exaggerated representations of human folly or vice, these characters have a tendency to be two-dimensional and show no signs of self-awareness or development during the course of the play. This is not completely true of *The School for Scandal*, which mixes burlesque with more sentimental comedy. Whilst Sir Oliver and Rowley are benevolent and good-natured throughout, we are asked to accept that both Sir Peter and Lady Teazle undergo changes of heart towards the end of the play. Sheridan shows this by Lady Teazle's contrition, her renunciation of 'the scandalous college' (V.3.187) and her apparent newfound happiness with her husband. Charles too reforms, though we are asked simply to take his word for it in the final lines of the play. With these exceptions, however, Sheridan's characters in the main show little real complexity or subtlety; his interests lay rather in exaggeration, comic situations and well-turned dialogue.

STRUCTURE

Sheridan follows the conventional five-act structure that would have been familiar to audiences of his time. The plot is set in motion in the opening scene and the scandal school are introduced. As the play progresses, Sheridan varies the scenes between more intimate conversations between small groups of characters and larger groups. He also maintains the pace by varying the length and tone of the scenes. After the long opening scene, in which characters continue to enter until there are seven actors on stage animatedly sharing the latest gossip, Scene 2 opens with Sir Peter alone, unburdening his heart to the audience and then in earnest discussion with Rowley – a mere 87 lines compared to the 366 lines of Act I Scene 1. Act II opens with a burst of verbal fireworks; there are still only two characters on stage but this time they are Sir Peter and Lady Teazle in furious quarrel. From that heated domestic scene we move again to a more public location, Lady Sneerwell's house, where the atmosphere is full of malicious gossip. Sheridan continues this variety to the end of the play, ensuring that the strands of his plot remain alive in the audience's memory as he builds towards the climax and introducing a new location and atmosphere in Act III with the high-spirited scenes in Charles' house, complete with drinking and a rousing song. This not only conveys the kind of merrymaking that has consumed Charles' money but was also intended by Sheridan as another memorable moment in the play over which he and his father-in-law (who composed the music) took some care; the song would have been accompanied by an orchestra in the original production. The pace within the longer scenes is also carefully controlled, as a examination of Act III Scene 1 will reveal: after some plotting of the test for the Surface brothers, Sir Peter is seen failing to control first Maria and then his wife. During the climax of this scene, the mood switches from apparently good-humoured recollections of their courtship to savagely **ironic** endearments until Lady Teazle turns on Sir Peter, overflowing with fury: 'You are a great bear, I'm sure, to abuse my relations' (III.1. 226). Sheridan then concludes with a comic note as she leaves with a laugh.

QUESTION

Why do you think Sheridan delays Charles' arrival on stage until Act III Scene 3 – about halfway through the play?

Although the quarrels between Sir Peter and Lady Teazle are in many ways the verbal high points of the play, the dramatic climax comes, following the traditional pattern, in Act IV with the 'screen scene' during which Sheridan skilfully brings together the key figures, unmasks deception (dramatically represented by the falling of the screen) and reveals their errors to the Teazles. The plot now proceeds to a satisfactory **denouement** in the final scene, in which the loose ends are tied up, Joseph is finally denounced, Lady Sneerwell is dismissed, Lady Teazle and her husband are reconciled and Charles is to marry Maria. Even here, whilst conforming to conventional structure and the taste for a sentimental conclusion, Sheridan shows his skill with the comic attack by the two brothers on Sir Oliver as they attempt to keep him out of sight. This final scene is also a reminder of the climax in Act IV Scene 3, with Lady Sneerwell and Snake dramatically brought on stage at key moments. Sir Peter makes this explicit with his reference to 'another French milliner!' (V.3.163) and 'Plot and counterplot, egad!' (V.3.182), though here his tone is amused and mocking, in contrast to the anger and misery he is shown to feel in Act IV.

An early biographer, having seen Sheridan's drafts, claimed that he was working on two plays and only brought them together at the last minute. In his view, Sheridan failed to fully integrate his plots involving on the one hand 'The Slanderers' (his early title for the scenes with the scandalmongers) and 'The Teazles'. The plots are interwoven, of course – Joseph's hypocrisy is the object of savage **satire** but also essential to the plot involving Lady Teazle, his brother and Maria. There is a sense in which the strands are kept apart; the scandalmongers dominate two early scenes (Act I Scene 1 and Act II Scene 2) and then do not reappear until Act V Scene 2, with only Lady Sneerwell making an appearance in the final scene. Sheridan almost certainly intended all along to join these sketches into a single play, though the existence of these early drafts gives a vivid insight into the way in which he combines satire with a story, creating a finished product that has at least the suggestion of a more serious moral message than the follies of scandal alone would convey.

QUESTION

How successfully do you think Sheridan maintains our interest in the plot right up to the end of the play?

LANGUAGE AND STYLE

The brilliance of Sheridan's dialogue was praised by the earliest critics. It is this, and the satirical uses to which he puts it, that has ensured the play's continuing popularity. The dialogue, of course, makes its full impact when skilfully delivered on stage, relying as all comedy does on timing, gesture and tone of voice as well as the right words in the script. The writer and politician Horace Walpole commented in 1780: 'I have read *The School for Scandal*; it is rapid and lively, but it is far from containing the wit I expected from seeing it acted' (Toynbee (ed.), *The Letters of Horace Walpole*, Volume 10, p. 82).

In the eighteenth century 'wit' meant more than just humour; it was applied to verbal brilliance, which by its brevity and accuracy produced comic surprise and, often, the revelation of truth. The poet Alexander Pope defined 'true wit' in his *Essay on Criticism* (1711) as 'What oft was thought, but ne'er so well expressed.' Sheridan himself employs this kind of epigrammatic wit in *The School for Scandal*; for example, Sir Peter remarks bitterly of Lady Sneerwell's set: 'Yes, egad, they are tenacious of reputation with a vengeance; for they don't choose anybody should have a character but themselves' (II.1.86–8). More often, however, Sheridan uses dialogue to show the true nature of the characters, whether for our amusement or for a more satirical purpose; at times, he seems to be revelling in the comedy of **repartee** in which each speaker seeks to outdo the other in witty retorts. Contrasted with these displays of wit are the characters who are marked by their plain speaking; occasionally, too, Sheridan resorts to the language of genuine feeling.

CHECK THE BOOK

'[T]he dialogue, from beginning to end, is a continued sparkling of polish and point' (Thomas Moore, *Memoirs of the Life of the Right Honourable Richard Brinsley Sheridan*, Longman, 1825, Volume 1, p. 247).

One of the most marked features of Sheridan's dialogue is the way he uses the characters' own words to reveal their true natures. 'Even Trip,' wrote Thomas Moore in 1825, '… is as pointed and shining as the rest, and has his master's wit, as he has his birth-day clothes, "with the gloss on"' (*Memoirs of the Life of the Right Honourable Richard Brinsley Sheridan*, Volume 1, p. 274). Sheridan is careful to vary the 'wit' he gives to his characters to suit their situations or the uses he wishes to make of them. Trip's talk is of clothes and loans, of 'point ruffles' and 'collateral security' (III.2.51). Mrs Candour's portrait is more satirical, as she condemns herself out of her own mouth. Garrulous in the extreme, Mrs Candour claims always to be wishing, she says, to 'think the best' whilst relishing the worst: 'By the bye, I hope 'tis not true that your brother is absolutely ruined?' (I.1.225–7). From the first moment she appears on stage in this scene she runs through a long list of reputations; Maria's comments, such as 'there are no grounds for that report' are unable to stem the flow (I.1.199). The male members of the scandal school are marked by their affectation and vanity; their wit is feeble and Sheridan makes them figures of fun rather than a serious threat: Sir Benjamin is praised for 'the epigram he wrote last week on Lady Frizzle's feather catching fire' (I.1.245–6).

CHECK THE BOOK

Alexander Pope's (1688–1744) poem, *The Rape of The Lock* (1714), about the act of cutting off a lock of a lady's hair, uses **satire** in a similar way to Sheridan, burlesquing the pretensions and petty niceties of the middle and upper classes.

Joseph's language is even more artfully developed to reveal the depths of his hypocrisy. His excessive civility to 'Mr Stanley' makes his insincerity obvious: 'I beg you ten thousand pardons for keeping you a moment ... Sir, I beg you will do me the honour to sit down. – I entreat you, sir'. As Sir Oliver says in an **aside**, 'Too civil by half' (V.1.40–5). Joseph, as has been noted already (see **Characterisation**), adopts formulaic expressions of sentiment when he wishes to impress, though Lady Sneerwell is contemptuous when it seems that he is 'going to be moral' in conversation with her (I.1.109). The pattern is so distinctive that Rowley is able to taunt Sir Peter with an imitation of Joseph at the end of the play: 'Nay, Sir Peter, he who once lays aside suspicion – ' (V.2.248). Compare this with Joseph's sentiments in the screen scene: 'the man who can break the laws of hospitality and attempt the wife of his friend … ' (IV.3.173–6). The satire is of course accentuated for the audience by the fact that Lady Teazle is hiding behind the screen, Joseph having just attempted the very thing he so sanctimoniously condemns. In the tradition of Shakespearian drama, Sheridan gives Joseph a more direct mode of speech when, as the villain, he speaks his mind to the audience: Lady Teazle 'must by no means be let into that secret [about his designs on Maria] – at least, till I have her more in my power' (IV.3.16–17).

Sheridan's skill at **repartee** is particularly evident in the two quarrel scenes between Sir Peter and Lady Teazle. In the first of these, for example, the old man's attempt to assert his authority is demonstrated to be futile by the way his wife turns his very first words against him:

> SIR PETER Lady Teazle, Lady Teazle, I'll not bear it!
> LADY TEAZLE Sir Peter, Sir Peter you may bear it or not, as you please; but I ought to have my own way in everything – and, what's more, I will too.
> (II.1.1–4)

This rapid interplay between the two continues as she picks up on his references to 'authority' and then 'extravagance'. What seems to him a reasonable view – that she ought not to buy expensive flowers in winter – becomes unreasonable when she turns this into a complaint against the climate for causing high prices. In each case, Sheridan increases the comic effect by endowing the couple with lavish exaggeration: he complains she spends 'as much to furnish your dressing-room with flowers in winter as would suffice to turn the Pantheon into a greenhouse and give a *fête champêtre* at Christmas!' and she replies, 'I'm sure I wish it was spring all the year round and that roses grew under one's feet!' (II.1.18–25). This sparring is repeated in their second quarrel in Act III Scene 1. After the argument has become increasingly heated (Lady Teazle always with the upper hand however), Sir Peter says he 'was a madman to marry you – a pert rural coquette ...', an insult she turns back on him with: 'And I am sure I was a fool to marry you – an old dangling bachelor ...' (III.1.231–5). It is a scene of pure linguistic table tennis, absolutely delightful to witness.

Sheridan sets against these displays of wit several characters distinguished by their plain speaking. Maria consciously rejects wit altogether: if to be witty is to 'to raise malicious smiles at the infirmities or misfortunes of those who have never injured us,' she says, 'Heaven grant me a double portion of dullness!' (II.2.186–9). Sir Peter is equally outspoken: 'no person should be permitted to kill characters or run down reputations, but qualified old maids and disappointed widows,' he remarks to Lady Sneerwell (who is, we already know, herself a 'disappointed widow', II.2.160–2). Charles, though more lively and better able to turn a phrase, also takes pride in the kind of blunt speaking that rejects hypocrisy: 'the plain state of the matter is this: I am an extravagant young fellow who want money to borrow.' Dubbing him 'Exceedingly frank,' Sir Oliver identifies that Charles is 'not a man of many compliments' (III.3.114–23). Having created in Joseph a hypocrite distinguished by his empty words, Sheridan illustrates the difference between words and actions in the way Charles sends money to Stanley as soon as he is able. Joseph's 'insidious arguments' and 'pretended passion' would have seduced Lady Teazle (IV.3.402–3) and even when confronted in the last scene, Joseph believes he can explain himself. In contrast, when Sir Oliver says: 'you could justify yourself *too*, I suppose?', Charles replies: 'Not that I know of' (V.3.123–5).

CHECK THE BOOK

In 1955, Kenneth Tynan, the theatre critic made the following observation: 'In writing plays, the ear is paramount; when that withers, everything withers' (*Theatrical Writings*, Nick Hern Books, 2007).

CHECK THE BOOK

An audio recording of *The School for Scandal* from the 1950s was reissued as a two-CD set in the EMI Classics for Pleasure series in 2006. The cast includes Cecil Parker, Harry Andrews, Alec Clunes, Claire Bloom and Dame Edith Evans.

QUESTION
Can you find further examples of witty dialogue in the play? One of the scenes involving the scandalmongers would be a good place to start.

If the displays of wit indicate Sheridan's debt to the Restoration comedies of playwrights such as Congreve, the implied preference for honest, direct speaking over artful wit is a sign of the growing emphasis on genuine emotions that was to find its expression in Wordsworth's preference for 'the real language of men' who 'being less under the influence of social vanity ... convey their feelings and notions in simple and unelaborated expressions' (Preface to *Lyrical Ballads*, 1800). The language of genuine feeling is, however, rare in *The School for Scandal*. When Sir Peter laments his state at the opening of the second scene, his feelings are not in doubt but Sheridan's tone is comic: ''Tis now six months since Lady Teazle made me the happiest of men – and I have been the miserablest dog since we committed matrimony' (I.2.1–4). More directly, Sir Oliver and Rowley speak openly in praise of Charles' 'benevolence' and with contempt for Joseph's sentiments. However, only in the last scene of the play does Sheridan use the kind of language that might have been found in sentimental comedies, when Charles says to Sir Oliver, 'I feel at this moment the warmest satisfaction in seeing you, my liberal benefactor' (V.3.141–2) and talks in the last lines of the 'virtuous path [Maria's] eyes illumine' (lines 245–6).

Sheridan's skill with dialogue was no doubt due at least in part to the particular circumstances of his education and his upbringing in the theatre. He would have learnt the art of rhetoric in his classical studies at school and he began training as a lawyer, where such skills were prized. More importantly he was taught grammar and oratory by his father, whose skills in teaching Scots the art of 'proper' English speech were rewarded by the freedom of the city of Edinburgh in 1761. In the artificial language of Joseph Surface, Sheridan shows how it is possible to disguise villainy by studied rhetoric but also, in the wisdom of Sir Oliver, that those of more honest outlook soon discern the difference between genuine sentiments and false ones. The dangers of misapplied rhetoric are demonstrated when Joseph attempts to persuade Lady Teazle that, now Sir Peter has become suspicious, 'the original compact is broke; and she owes it to the honour of her sex to outwit him' (IV.3.49–50). In this scene Joseph uses the rhetoric of persuasion in a series of fallacious arguments ('your husband should never be deceived in you; and in that case, it becomes you to be frail in compliment to his discernment', lines 54–6), rhetorical questions ('What makes you thoughtless in your conduct ...?', line 63) and plausible maxims ('Prudence, like experience, must be paid for', lines 81–2) to support his false conclusion. Lady Teazle has the wit to reply with a nicely balanced pair of paradoxes even though it is clear that she sees the immorality of his proposal (IV.3.76–7). The danger of such cunning rhetoric is indicated by the fact that it is only the unexpected arrival of Lady Teazle's husband that prevents Joseph from prevailing. Sheridan uses the rhetorical device of a triple accusation from Sir Oliver, Sir Peter and Lady Teazle to emphasise Joseph's complete unmasking in the final scene; Lady Teazle even resorts to legal terminology as she delivers the final blow: 'And if the gentleman pleads not guilty to these, pray let him call *me* to his character' (V.3.108–9).

CONTEXT

Following his two duels with Mathews, Sheridan's father despatched him in 1772 to Waltham Abbey in Essex to study law. The next year he was entered as a student at the Middle Temple, the first step to becoming a barrister. Although he proceeded no further in his studies, his legal background, along with his training in elocution and oratory by his father, stood him in good stead both in the theatre and in the House of Commons. His rhetoric in the impeachment and prosecution of Warren Hastings reduced most of the distinguished audience to tears.

course none the worse for this latter fact; it is only less imaginative.

CONTEXT

George Bernard Shaw (1856–1950) was an Irish playwright, essayist and socialist. At the time of his review of *The School for Scandal* he was making his living as a critic. He wrote over sixty plays and was awarded the Nobel Prize for Literature. Among his plays are *Mrs Warren's Profession* (1893), *Major Barbara* (1905), *Saint Joan* (1923) and *Pygmalion* (1912) (later made into the musical *My Fair Lady*).

By 1896, George Bernard Shaw was complaining that the morality of the play was so hopelessly dated as to be unacceptable, though he too praised the dialogue: 'Sheridan wrote for the actor as Handel wrote for the singer, setting him a combination of strokes which, however difficult some of them may be to execute finely, are familiar to all practised actors as the strokes which experience has shewn to be proper to the nature and capacity of the stage-player as a dramatic instrument'.

During the twentieth century the play continued to be popular on stage, though its critical reputation suffered; Restoration plays were preferred for their greater sexual frankness and supposed realism. Jack Durant wrote in 1973: '*The School for Scandal* has never really fared well with the critics. They have seen it, of course, as a splendid theatrical masterpiece, "an acting play" and "a play for actors", but as morally insightful art they have granted it little merit, complaining, for example, that it "teaches no lesson and points no distinctive moral", that is emphasises "what is admirable, what is 'virtuous', rather than keeping our attention upon what is ridiculous", that it "clicks its heels before conventional morality", inveighing only against "what is demonstrably safe".' Seeking to rescue the play's reputation, Durant compares the portrait of Joseph in the play with Sheridan's speech eleven years later attacking Warren Hastings for abuses in India. 'The main thematic issues of the play ... turn not upon who gets the money and the girl but upon why, in the moral scheme of things, virtuous motives will eventually triumph over vicious ones' (from *Studies in Burke and His Time*, cited in Davison (ed.), *Sheridan: Comedies*, pp. 180–8).

John Loftis, in his seminal work, *Sheridan and the Drama of Georgian England*, written in 1977, exactly two hundred years after *The School for Scandal* made its theatrical debut, praises the dialogue of the play and the particular success of the malicious characters. While the romance plot gives the play shape, he argues, it makes much less of a lasting impression than the sinister scandal school whose evil intentions dominate the tone, if not the text, of the play:

> In a full experience of the play, the satirical dialogue, and the sharply realized hypocrites who speak it, create the dominant impression. The rivalry for Maria – whose presence on stage is minimal for one who is the matrimonial prize – does indeed provide the framing action, with a 'beginning, middle, and end'. Yet if our sympathies are engaged on behalf of Charles and Maria, we leave a performance of the play, not with a benign pleasure in seeing benevolence rewarded, but rather with a disturbing recollection of malicious persons who embody ubiquitous qualities of mind as well as of heart. (p. 87)

Recent productions have often attempted a similar link to Sheridan's world, whether it was the 'itch beneath the powder' that Tyrone Guthrie sought to convey as far back as 1937 by emphasising the minor parts and the servants, or the lavish spectacle of news sheets arriving on stage that preceded the 1990 National Theatre production in London. Declan Donnellan's 1998 Royal Shakespeare Theatre production even had the Prince of Wales on stage as the play's prime audience, with Sheridan at his side hoping for advancement. Lady Sneerwell, in a reference to Sheridan's background, spoke the Prologue in an Irish accent. In the screen scene (Act IV Scene 3), Joseph and Lady Teazle gradually removed items of clothing as their dialogue progressed, in an explicit depiction of the seduction Sheridan implies is about to take place. This confident approach to the text indicates that *The School for Scandal* still has the ability to excite directors and audiences over two hundred years after its first production.

WWW. CHECK THE NET

Reviews of several recent productions can be found on the Internet. Try searching for 'school for scandal review' and see what entries come up. One example is the Yorkshire Bridge Theatre's 2005 production reviewed on the BBC website (**www.bbc.co.uk**) which includes a photograph of cast members in costume.

CONTEMPORARY APPROACHES

Although, as indicated in the previous section, the play continues to be produced, often in innovative ways, there is little readily available recent critical work on *The School for Scandal*. The play has remained alive for directors and actors but does not seem to have offered much material of interest to theorists. The following

MARXISM continued

CHECK THE BOOK
One of the best known examples of Marxist criticism is Raymond Williams' *Culture and Society* (Chatto and Windus, 1958).

A Marxist critic might therefore begin by looking at the means of production for *The School for Scandal* – starting with the theatre. As is discussed in the section on **New historicism**, Drury Lane depended on royal patronage and also represented a considerable financial investment for its owners. Of the £10,000 Sheridan had to find for his share of the patent, he needed to borrow £7,700 from Dr James Ford, one of the other shareholders, and raise £1,000 in mortgages (his account of money lending in the play was clearly based on personal experience). The owners could not afford to upset either the monarchy or the audience. That audience, up to 3,611 a night in the late eighteenth century, included a growing middle class. Out of a London population in the 1770s of 750,000, about 12,000 went to the theatre each week.

With this in mind, the play could be seen as reinforcing conventional social and moral values such as loyalty to family and class and obedience to social structures. Marriage is clearly shown as being an economic relationship as much as, if not more than, a romantic one, as is demonstrated when Sir Peter requests a kiss after he has given his wife £200 with the financial term: 'seal me a bond', and she replies with another: 'my note of hand will do as well' (III.1.177–9). Charles is depicted as a social parasite, depending on an expanding capitalist system of loans (themselves exploitative) and finally rescued by the arrival of the wealth his uncle has gained by a colonial adventure in India (which itself could be the subject of further comment as an indication of the expansion of the British Empire).

There is much more in the play that lends itself to social or economic scrutiny. Sheridan, adopting long-standing stage conventions, does not show any of his major characters working for their money, though Charles is desperate to raise it, Joseph wishes to marry Maria for her money, Lady Teazle needs to ask her husband for all her money and the plot hinges on who will receive Sir Oliver's 'bullion – rupees, pagodas' (V.1.68). The scandalmongers' vices are the product of their idleness; not needing to work, they entertain themselves with slander. Poverty, where it is seen in the figure of Stanley, is hardly real as he is in fact the wealthy Sir Oliver in disguise; in any case, he is introduced simply as a test of the brothers' generosity in order to prove who is worthy to receive more money, not as a spur to their social consciousness or, arguably, that of the audience. Trip, is the one genuine indicator of the effect of economics on individuals: we see him working and even find out what he earns (and how paltry it is in comparison to the sums Lady Teazle and Charles fritter away). We also see that he has been drawn into the capitalist economic system, mortgaging the clothes he expects to acquire from his master's wardrobe against the annuity he tries to raise from Moses. However, Sheridan implies there is ultimately no one to blame for this extravagance except Trip himself, as he is as indulgent and unrepentant as the rest of them.

FEMINISM

Feminist criticism covers a wide range of approaches. These explore the representation of women in literature, the gender politics and power relations depicted in texts, and examine the ideological bases of other critical approaches that sideline women as writers or readers.

A feminist approach to *The School for Scandal* might draw on some of the critical approaches outlined above, such as the economic dependence of women on men. Lady Teazle cannot achieve financial independence unless Sir Peter dies or gives her a separate allowance – either way, she is reliant on him. It could also be inferred from the play that she only married Sir Peter because of his wealth, since he was old enough to be her father. When he says she 'never had such an offer before', she reminds him of 'Sir Tivy Terrier', whose 'estate is just as good as yours' (III.1.238-41). Money, in other words, is what matters when it comes to choosing a husband, not the love that is sentimentally claimed to rule the hearts of Maria and Lady Teazle herself. Once she has money, Lady Teazle spends it on 'feminine' extravagances – flowers in winter, a coach and powdered footmen – that show her conformity to society's expectations now that she is a kept 'woman of fashion' (II.1.5). This seems to illustrate Mary Wollstonecraft's contention in *A Vindication of the Rights of Woman* (1792) that 'to rise in the world, and to have the liberty of running from pleasure to pleasure,' middle-class women 'must marry advantageously, and to this object their time is sacrificed, and their persons often legally prostituted.'

CONTEXT

Mary Wollstonecraft (1759–89) won fame for promoting the rights of women in the late eighteenth century. She wrote prose tracts and fictional narratives to highlight the plight of women of all classes. For more on Wollstonecraft, see **Historical background**.

CHECK THE BOOK

'The women in the play are set apart and regarded as absolutely outside the region of free judgment in which men act,' said George Bernard Shaw in review of a production in 1896, adding that the quite different moral standards for men and women mean '*The School for Scandal* dates on the Woman Question almost as badly as the *Taming of the Shrew.*'

The importance of reputation and the different moral standards applied to men and women might form another strand in a feminist approach to the play. Sheridan, in his *Ode to the Genius of Scandal*, portrays slander as a danger to women; it is a 'weeping maid' who is ruined in his poem, just as Lady Teazle fears she will be 'ruined' by her discovery in Joseph's library. The scandal school, whilst it includes two men, is dominated by women and their main topic of gossip is other women. The achievements or qualities of their targets are of no concern, only their reputations and their appearance. This might suggest that Lady Sneerwell and Mrs Candour are only tools in society's drive to police women and keep them in their place. For men, the play suggests, the standards are different; while a woman's good reputation is essential in protecting her from ignominy, Charles' dissolute lifestyle is looked on with indulgence by the men. As Sir Oliver says, 'I am not sorry he has run out of the course a little' (II.3.74–5), suggesting that a little immorality does a man no harm. On the other hand, it seems only a woman can guide him into the way of righteousness. Can we take seriously Charles' vow to Maria that 'Thou still must rule, because I will obey,' in such a male-dominated world as this (V.3.245–8)? He has after all taken it for granted that she will marry him the next day despite her silence. Maria therefore passes seamlessly from the power of her guardian to the authority of her husband – making it clear that she lives in a patriarchal society.

An alternative approach would credit Sheridan with more sensitivity to the position of women. Whilst the play upholds the moral code of his time, his female characters are at least as important as the males. Although Maria is the kind of passive heroine who is seen as the prize for the victorious hero, Lady Sneerwell controls her own fortunes and Sheridan has created in Lady Teazle a woman with a lively independence that could be a reflection of the increasing influence of women as their economic fortunes grew and the Romantic movement took hold. Responses to such an approach depend on assessing how much genuine freedom Lady Teazle has at the end of the play. Has she established an equal relationship with her husband or is she still obliged to depend upon him for everything? Colman's Epilogue to the play seems ambivalent; whilst Mrs Abington (still dressed as Lady Teazle) advises the women in the audience 'No more in vice or folly to engage', the picture she paints of her 'dismal doom' in the country sounds unappealing and her tone **ironic** (lines 49, 18). Is this the portrait of an empowered woman who chooses her fate, or of a victim of a male-dominated society? A feminist interpretation might well view eighteenth-century marriage as a kind of financial slavery that subjugated female independence to a false sentimental ideal.

QUESTION

Do any of the critical approaches described here shed new light on the play for you? Are there other critical approaches that, in your opinion, might offer more helpful insights?

PART FIVE

BACKGROUND

RICHARD BRINSLEY SHERIDAN'S LIFE AND WORKS

Sheridan's family could lay claim to learning and professional success, though not to wealth. The O'Sheridans, from Cavan in Ireland, had converted from Catholicism in the seventeenth century and become part of the Protestant ascendancy – that is, the religious minority whose power derived from British rule. Richard Brinsley Sheridan's grandfather, Dr Thomas Sheridan, was a clergyman and schoolmaster with an interest in language, mathematics and the theatre, and a close friend of the poet, satirist and clergyman Jonathan Swift, best known as the author of *Gulliver's Travels* (1726). Swift was godfather to Richard Brinsley Sheridan's father, another Thomas Sheridan, who became an actor, playwright and educator. For a while Thomas Sheridan was a close friend of Dr Johnson, complier of the famous dictionary. Thomas Sheridan had established himself as the successful actor-manager of Smock Alley Theatre in Dublin by the time Richard Brinsley was born in 1751. The exact date of his birth is not recorded, though it was probably in September; he was christened on 4 November with the name Thomas Brinsley Sheridan. It is possible that this was a mistake by the parish clerk, though he may have been given the name of an older brother, who had died the previous year at the age of three. In any event, he was soon known as Richard, the name of uncles on both his mother's and his father's side.

CONTEXT

One dissenting voice in the chorus of praise for *The School for Scandal* was that of Thomas Sheridan, his father: 'Talk of the merit of Dick's play, there's nothing in it,' he said sourly, 'he had but to dip the pen in his own heart and he'd find there the characters of both Joseph and Charles Surface' (cited in Kelly, *Richard Brinsley Sheridan: A Life*, p. 82).

The uncertainty that a theatrical life can bring was experienced by the family when protests over the suspension of the Irish Parliament by the government in London led to riots which closed the theatre and his parents and elder brother Charles moved to London, leaving the three-year-old Richard in Dublin. For the next eight years he was frequently separated from his family and in 1762 was sent as a boarding pupil to Harrow School. He never returned to Ireland after 1759 but he did not forget his Irish roots; years later he was taking a stand for the rights of Catholics in Ireland and he even became a candidate for election to the Irish Parliament in 1807. Richard's early years at Harrow were unhappy, though later he made some strong friendships and left with fond memories of the school and his teachers. His parents, concerned that his father might be arrested by creditors and seeking to live more cheaply, moved to France in 1764, leaving Richard at school, where he was to learn two years later of his mother's death. Thomas Sheridan returned to London and set about educating his sons in grammar and oratory, with additional lessons in Latin, mathematics and fencing. Thomas had by this time achieved some fame with the publication of the first English pronunciation dictionary and was offering to teach elocution to those wanting, for example, to remove the 'barbarisms' of regional accents; he included some of the Scots nobility amongst his students.

CONTEXT

Sheridan left his name carved in the Fourth Form Room at Harrow School, where it can still be seen, and the school later took pride in his achievements. The poet Byron recalled how, when he was at the school thirty-eight years later, 'we used to show his name – R. B. Sheridan, 1765 – as an honour to the walls' (Byron, Letter to Thomas Moore, cited in Kelly, *Richard Brinsley Sheridan: A Life*, p 21).

The family moved to Bath, where Thomas Sheridan set up an academy. Thomas had intended his son for the law, but Richard had by now determined to make a career as a writer. In 1770 he also first made the acquaintance of the Linley family and in particular of the beautiful Elizabeth, then only sixteen but already famous for her beauty and for her singing voice. It seems that it was his elder brother who first fell in love with her, though he was not alone in his admiration. But she was not free to make her own choice; her father first made an arrangement that she would marry Walter Long, a man (rather like Sir Peter in *The School for Scandal*) about thirty years older than her. It seems that Elizabeth begged her father to release her from this; at all events, the engagement was broken off, though the affair soon became the subject of a play by Samuel Foote called *The Maid of Bath*. Elizabeth, for all her success, apparently hated singing in public and sometimes fainted during or after performances, so the added attention must have been extremely unwelcome. Worse was to come. Captain Thomas Mathews, despite being married, pursued Elizabeth, attempting to seduce her and threatening to blacken her name around the town if she did not succumb. In her distress, she decided to take refuge in a convent and asked the Sheridan sisters, with whom she was good friends, to assist her. Richard took on the role of her protector and in March 1772 he escorted her to France. On the way, he declared

CONTEXT

Sheridan was amused by the reports in the papers after his second duel with Mathews: 'Let me see what they report of me today; I wish to know whether I am dead or alive'. This sensational reporting echoes the accounts of the supposed duel in Act V Scene 2.

CONTEXT

Sheridan determined that Elizabeth would not sing in public, partly because she hated performing but also because a gentleman did not allow his wife to sing for money. She fulfilled two final engagements (as 'the celebrated Mrs Sheridan') once she was married; the Sunday after the last one, she ostentatiously placed her £100 fee in the church collection plate.

his love for her and, perhaps in part to protect her reputation, they underwent a Catholic marriage near Calais. As neither of them had then attained the age of majority (twenty-one at the time) the marriage was not legally binding, however, and when they returned to England, their parents sought to keep them apart. Thomas Linley's concerns were partly financial – Elizabeth had been earning large sums for the family – but also from a desire to protect his daughter's reputation, for the affair had become a sensation in the small, gossip-hungry society of Bath. Mathews had contributed to this by insulting 'Mr Richard S' in the *Bath Chronicle*; Sheridan responded by challenging him to a duel, which he won. Mathews was forced to issue a retraction in print, but it seems he was not satisfied and he later repeated his insults. This led to a second, more serious duel in which Sheridan was seriously injured. This indication of the sincerity of his feelings for Elizabeth probably helped reconcile at least Elizabeth's family to the relationship and they were officially married in 1773. Sheridan was soon working with his new father-in-law and his talented children; his own father was more intractable. Although Thomas Sheridan later played a part in the management of Drury Lane, he appears to have been as obstinate as Sir Peter Teazle in his preference for his elder son, and it was only towards the end of his life that he became reconciled to the son who had so brilliantly taken on his role of manager and writer – and in the process transformed himself, as his father never did, into an celebrated member of London society.

Sheridan sought to establish himself as a writer and with his family background in the theatre it is not surprising that he should turn his hand to a play. Within a relatively short time he had convinced the management of Covent Garden Theatre (one of the two Royal Patent theatres in London) to accept his proposal for *The Rivals*. Although it was his first work for the theatre and the first night was not a success, Sheridan realised his errors, shortening and amending the play so that subsequent performances were greeted with acclaim. The plot is slight and so full of incredible devices that it is clear Sheridan was writing a **burlesque**, mocking the pretensions of the Bath society he had observed during his stay there. The heroine, Lydia Languish, has had her head turned by romantic novels to such an extent that she will only marry a penniless lover, so although Jack

Absolute's father has determined that his son will marry Lydia, Jack has to pretend to be poor Ensign Beverley to persuade her to see him. Sir Anthony Absolute is a stock tyrannical father, with an added hostility to women's education (perhaps an echo of his mother's own father). Mrs Malaprop, probably Sheridan's most famous creation, is an example of mangled articulation and poor education; such was her fame that 'malapropism' became the name for the comic misuse of a word. There is also a second pair of lovers, with Faulkland as ridiculous as Lydia, though in his case the weakness is a pathological sense of his own unworthiness in the face of Julia's constancy. Sheridan throws in wily servants, a hot-blooded Irishman who mistakes letters from Mrs Malaprop as being from Lydia, a country lover attempting to acquire the graces of society and, as a climax, comic duel scenes.

Sheridan had begun his dramatic career with style and the next few years were marked with success. His short **farce** *St Patrick's Day* had only a slight success in May 1775 but *The Duenna*, which followed that November, was astonishingly successful. It is a comic opera, set in Spain, with a typically outlandish plot involving once again a tyrannical father, lovers eloping, confused identities and a duel. With music arranged by Sheridan's father- and brother-in-law, it was immediately popular and provided welcome financial security to the young family – his first son, Thomas, was born just four days after the first night of *The Duenna.* The following year, Sheridan was sufficiently well established to win the support of Garrick and buy part of the retiring actor-manger's share in the Theatre Royal, Drury Lane, though he had to borrow extensively to do so. Sheridan was now manager of one of the capital's two royal theatres, both a great achievement and a responsibility. He needed to ensure the theatre met its considerable expenses by attracting large audiences. His adaptation of Vanbrugh's *The Relapse* as *A Trip to Scarborough* in 1777 was not well received and so a great deal depended on the first night of *The School for Scandal* on 8 May – late in the season. Sheridan had, however, learnt a large amount in his short time as a playwright and his reputation was well deserved – the first night audience was packed with fashionable members of society and the play was a tremendous success.

CONTEXT

Theodore Hook recounts that two days before the first performance of *The Critic* the final scene was not written. 'His father-in-law ... hit upon a stratagem. A night rehearsal of *The Critic* was ordered ... King [the stage manager and the original Sir Peter] ... begged he would step into the second green-room. Accordingly, Sheridan went, and there found a table, with pens, ink, and paper, a good fire, an armed chair, and two bottles of claret, with a dish of anchovy sandwiches. The moment he got into the room, King stepped out, and locked the door ... Sheridan ate the anchovies, finished the claret, wrote the scene and laughed heartily at the ingenuity of the contrivance.'

CONTEXT

'Rotten boroughs' were constituencies for the English Parliament which could elect MPs even though they had few or no inhabitants. A 'pocket borough' was one in which one person or family could dictate how the votes were cast; the election was therefore 'in the pocket' of the patron. Both were abolished by the Reform Act of 1832. By contrast, Stafford, which elected Sheridan as MP in 1780, was relatively democratic, having about 320 electors, most of them tradesmen.

With success at least temporarily assured, Sheridan's attention turned, as he seems to have long intended, to politics. He wrote one more play still occasionally performed today, *The Critic* of 1779, a short 'after-piece' intended to follow the main five-act play. It is a **burlesque** of the contemporary taste for spectacle and **tragedy** on the stage, with a mocking picture of the sentimental dramatist Richard Cumberland in the character of Sir Fretful Plagiary. Sheridan was elected as Member of Parliament for Stafford in 1780 and thereafter his career was in the House of Commons rather than the theatre. He remained involved in the management of the theatre, relying on it for most of his income as MPs had no salary at that time. He wrote one more play, *Pizarro*, an adaptation of a German melodrama, in 1799; its considerable success at the time indicated that he had not lost his dramatic skills. A tragedy and historical spectacular, *Pizarro* tells of the Spanish conquest of Peru in ways that clearly appealed to audiences at a time when Britain was threatened with invasion by France.

The remainder of Sheridan's life was as remarkable, and in many ways at least as distinguished, as the literary career for which he is now mainly remembered. As his major plays were already written, however, this part of his life is of less interest to the literary scholar and only a brief outline will be given here; there are two good modern biographies for those wishing to learn more (see **Further reading**). Sheridan was a Member of Parliament for thirty-two years, where he put the rhetorical skills he had learned from his father and from his time in the theatre to good use. His speeches for the impeachment and trial of Warren Hastings in 1787 and 1788 were acclaimed as pinnacles of the orator's art, even though the case was dismissed. Sheridan was a Whig, a liberal and supporter of freedoms and rights in a period when liberty was threatened. Repressive laws had been introduced to protect the government and monarchy against unrest during the years of the American and French Revolutions and the wars with France. Although he was, with Charles James Fox, the most prominent Whig politician of the time, most of the period was spent in opposition and he only held minor government offices for short intervals; unlike many politicians of the time he refused to accept positions for money that would compromise his independence. He spoke in favour of the abolition of the slave trade, arguing that it should be accompanied by the freeing of slaves in British colonies (shamefully, this plea was ignored when the slave trade was abolished by Britain in 1807) and he took an active interest in Irish affairs. His brother Charles was a Member of the Irish Parliament for many years and Sheridan sought to win greater freedoms for the Catholic majority in Ireland, though this was firmly opposed by the king. Sheridan became good friends with the Prince of Wales and had to perform a delicate balancing act between defending the prince against his political enemies (especially when the king suffered from his periodic bouts of insanity) in order to keep alive hopes of power when the prince ascended the throne, whilst at the same maintaining his independence. In 1807, having failed to retain his seat as Member of Parliament for Westminster, Sheridan had to accept the offer from the Prince of Wales of Illchester, a 'rotten borough' where the small number of voters was controlled by a wealthy patron.

Although his marriage had begun happily, Sheridan later adopted some of the practices of the fashionable society he had **satirised** in *The School for Scandal.* He became well known for his drinking and had a number of love affairs; it was probably these that drove Elizabeth to take a lover of her own, Lord Edward Fitzgerald, whose child she bore in 1792, not long before her own death. Sheridan insisted for the child's sake on bringing Mary up as his own daughter and was distraught when she died only seventeen months old. In 1795 he married again, to Esther Ogle, known as 'Hecca', daughter of the Dean of Winchester. She was nineteen, he was forty-three. Although she was extravagant and their marriage later endured strains, it seems, in another echo of *The School for Scandal*, that they were in love. Sheridan continued to hold a share in Drury Lane, which had been rebuilt to accommodate an even larger audience, but a fire of 1809 saw the theatre's complete destruction, to Sheridan's considerable cost. He had always been, like Charles in *The School for Scandal*, generous, not to say extravagant, with money and once he lost his parliamentary seat in 1812 he was no longer protected from arrest for his numerous debts. Although he enjoyed the friendship of the much younger Lord Byron during this time, he was unable to keep his creditors at bay for long and had to spend some periods in debtors' prisons until

CONTEXT

'It is said that, as he sat in the Piazza Coffee-house, during the fire [at Drury Lane in 1809], taking some refreshment, a friend of his having remarked on the philosophical calmness with which he bore his misfortune, Sheridan answered: "A man may surely be allowed to take a glass of wine *by his own fireside.*"' (Thomas Moore, *Memoirs of the Life of the Right Honourable Richard Brinsley Sheridan*, Volume 2, p. 231).

friends could raise money to release him. The bailiffs were apparently in the downstairs room of his house when he died in July 1816 at the age of sixty-five. He was buried in Poets' Corner in Westminster Abbey with a lavish funeral that contrasted sharply with the poverty of his final days.

CONTEXT

Initially *The School for Scandal* was refused a licence by the Lord Chamberlain. Benjamin Hopkins objected that the portrayal of Moses was an attack on him. Hopkins was a Christian alleged to lend money to under-age borrowers in return for crippling annuities on the property they might inherit. Sheridan was able to persuade the Lord Chamberlain that the attack was merely 'a matter of general satire' and the play went ahead as planned (cited in O'Toole, *A Traitor's Kiss*, pp. 128–9).

HISTORICAL BACKGROUND

A glance at the **Chronology** later in this section will reveal the turbulent times through which Sheridan lived. For most of the period from 1776 when Sheridan, fresh from the triumph of *The Rivals*, became a shareholder in Drury Lane to the end of his life, Britain was at war. For much of that time he was in Parliament, involved in constant efforts to gain or retain power, to resist tyranny and defend freedom. At times he was even at risk of treason charges himself. It was not surprising that contemporary politicians such as his rival William Pitt and his ally Fox died young; the pressures on a political system ill adapted to the times were enormous. Sheridan, despite his often-mocked fondness for drink, was a great survivor and by the end of his career must have seemed like a figure from another age. The fashions that he mentions as new in *The Rivals* and *The School for Scandal* were themselves now antique.

WWW. CHECK THE NET

The pages covering Tate Britain's 2007 exhibition on Hogarth provide useful background information on the painter as well as links to his works. Go to **www.tate.org.uk** and search for Hogarth.

Despite Sheridan's stated wish to keep politics out of the theatre, it is possible to hear some echoes of the times in his plays, though on many aspects he is silent. His comedies concern themselves largely with the follies of that small group called 'society'; they may not be wealthy landowners but they appear to have private incomes and their concerns are amusement, fashion, reputation and making good marriages. There is no record in the plays of the chimney sweepers and orphans that the London engraver and poet William Blake was writing about at the same time, nor even of the disorderly scenes depicted by the great **satiric** artist Hogarth, though Sheridan must have seen these as he walked about the city. It is not that he was ignorant of poverty; he kept detailed accounts of the theatre at Drury Lane and knew that whilst the best actors might earn large sums, other employees were less fortunate. When the theatre burnt down in 1809, he wrote to the company: 'Keep in your remembrance even the poor sweepers of the stage, who, with their children, must starve, if not protected by our fostering care.' The city of London was expanding rapidly as the industrial revolution gathered momentum and trade increased to the expanding British Empire. Sheridan makes passing reference to this in *The School for Scandal*; Sir Oliver has made his fortune as a 'nabob' in India. This seems merely to be a convenient source of wealth, though Sheridan's later defence of the Begums of Oudh in the trial of Warren Hastings reveals that at least by then he was aware of the greed and exploitation that was the source of much of the 'Indian gold' then flowing into Britain. The play also reminds its audience of the realities of economics; for those without great wealth, the financial system might provide loans but at a high price. Debt was a harsh fate for the careless, the extravagant or, like Mr Stanley, the unfortunate.

This was also a period of great political ferment as fresh ideas about liberty were gaining ground throughout Europe and America. Sheridan was aware of these and largely supported the American colonies' desire for independence. He, like many liberal thinkers of the time, was in also favour of the French people's desire to shake off the yolk of tyranny. Only when the French Revolution turned bloody and threatened Britain did he voice opposition, though even then he was prepared to defend the principle of freedom when it was dangerous to voice such views. He was constantly attempting to better the lot of those who lived in his native Ireland. This was also a time when the position of women was increasingly coming under scrutiny; Sheridan may have mocked the sentimental novels devoured by Lydia Languish in *The Rivals* but his own mother had written one and other women writers were beginning to make their voices heard. In 1792, Mary Wollstonecraft's influential *A Vindication of the Rights of Woman*, demanding equal rights with men, was published. Sheridan was friendly with the philosopher William Godwin, who married Wollstonecraft in 1797. In an interesting reflection of the world Sheridan depicts in *The School for Scandal*, Mary Wollstonecraft complained in *A Vindication of the Rights of Woman* that middle-class women at the time were being educated to seek 'pleasure as the main purpose of existence', to the

CONTEXT

Warren Hastings was accused of committing a wide range of crimes during his governorship of India. These included corruption, extortion, starting unjust wars and other abuses of power. Although he was acquitted, the trial ruined his reputation and his finances.

CONTEXT

A 'Bluestocking' (or 'blue stocking') is a woman who is interested in serious academic subjects; the term was often used in a disparaging way. The term originates in the evening parties held by a number of educated women from the 1750s in which card playing, then the principal recreation (as Mrs Abington indicates by her references in the Epilogue), was replaced by conversations on literary and philosophical subjects. Many who attended dressed informally, giving rise to the name – at least one gentleman attended dressed in blue worsted stockings as opposed to formal black silk.

detriment of their intellect and their freedom. Groups of cultivated and intellectual women were however establishing their own networks. Although mockingly dubbed 'Bluestockings', they were on occasions joined by men of letters such as Horace Walpole and Dr Johnson. The writer Hannah More describes one such gathering in 1775, two years before *The School for Scandal* was first produced: 'I have been at Mrs Boscawen's. Mrs Montagu, Mrs Carter, Mrs Chapone, and myself only were admitted. We spent the time, not as wits, but as reasonable creatures; better characters, I trow. The conversation was sprightly but serious.' In her reference to 'wits' it is possible to recognise a deliberate distancing from the activities of the kind of 'scandalous college' of which Lady Sneerwell is president.

LITERARY BACKGROUND

COMEDY, SATIRE AND SENTIMENT

Sheridan was thoroughly grounded in the theatre and produced many plays by earlier dramatists at Drury Lane. In his first six weeks as manager he staged three comedies by the Restoration dramatist William Congreve, the last of which, *The Way of the World*, dated from 1700, and he followed these with his own adaptation of Vanbrugh's *The Relapse* from 1696. His audiences, much larger and more middle class than those of the previous century, were however less willing to accept what they saw as the lax moral standards of an earlier age and some alterations had to be made – this change in taste can be seen also in the avoidance of explicit reference to sexual misconduct in *The School for Scandal*, though of course this is implied when Lady Teazle visits Joseph alone in his library in Act IV Scene 3. The earlier comedies Sheridan produced relied, as he did himself, as much on wit as on comic situations. Sheridan allied himself with his contemporary Oliver Goldsmith (also born in Ireland) in championing 'laughing comedy' over 'the sentimental muse' (see **Dramatic techniques: Sentimental and laughing comedy**), while Garrick wrote a Prologue to Goldsmith's *She Stoops to Conquer* of 1773 in which he protested at the taste for exaggeratedly emotional moral drama:

Pray would you know the reason why I'm crying?
The comic muse, long sick, is now a-dying!
And if she goes, my tears will never stop ...

Garrick concludes: 'I give it up – morals won't do for me.' Rather than simply adopting the contemporary trend for a greater moral seriousness, Sheridan sought to give voice to older comic traditions and retain a sense of lightness and wit. His **satire** invites the audience to laugh at characteristics and vices they would have recognised in their midst; at the time, the actors would have been wearing similar costumes to the audiences' own clothes, which would be clearly visible in the light of the candles that burned in the auditorium throughout the performance. Satire has a long history in and outside the theatre; commentators in Sheridan's day noticed similarities not only with the drama of the English Restoration but also with the plays of the French satiric dramatists, who sought to expose hypocrisy and vice through humour. The title of Molière's play *L'école des femmes* (*The School for Wives*) of 1662 may be echoed in *The School for Scandal*.

In Britain, the earlier part of the eighteenth century had produced several satirical prose writers, the most famous of whom was Thomas Sheridan's godfather, Jonathan Swift. Swift's *Gulliver's Travels*, far from being a children's fable, is actually a savage attack on human failings, to the extent that the narrator ends up preferring to live with horses. Sheridan would have read Swift; the complete works were in his father's library. The earlier part of the century had also seen the rise of the English novel and there are some striking parallels between *The School for Scandal* and *Tom Jones* by Henry Fielding, published a couple of years before Sheridan was born. Fielding had been a successful dramatist until his comedies so upset the Prime Minister, Robert Walpole, that he passed the Stage Licensing Act in 1737. This Act effectively outlawed political satire from the stage and Fielding turned to writing fiction. (The Act also granted a monopoly to Drury Lane and Covent Garden from which Sheridan himself, of course, later benefited – see **Theatre in the late eighteenth century**). The eponymous hero of *Tom Jones* (1749) is handsome, brave, generous and well meaning but not always moral: '... though he did not always act rightly, yet he never did otherwise

CHECK THE BOOK

Mr Dangle, in *The Critic*, complains about the moral fastidiousness of audiences in Sheridan's time: 'No double-entendre, no smart innuendo admitted; even Vanbrugh and Congreve obliged to undergo a bungling reformation!' (Act I Scene 1).

CONTEXT

The title of Molière's play may have been even fresher in Sheridan's mind with the publication of an adaptation of *The School for Wives* by Hugh Kelly (1739–77) in 1773. Though Kelly claimed to have borrowed only the title from the earlier play, there were in fact many similarities in the plot.

without feeling and suffering for it' (Chapter 6). If Tom resembles Charles in *The School for Scandal*, the odiously hypocritical and scheming Blifil (finally revealed to be Tom's brother) is the Joseph Surface of Fielding's novel. There is also a tyrannical squire who, very like Sir Peter, forbids his beautiful daughter to see Tom – until he becomes convinced of the young man's generosity and good parentage (and therefore wealth) at the end of the novel.

Sheridan was writing in a tradition known as the **comedy of manners**. This genre deals with the relationships and intrigues of figures in a sophisticated society and relies for a great deal of its comic effect on the wit of the dialogue. An example from the Restoration period that has interesting parallels with *The School for Scandal* is William Wycherley's *The Country Wife* of 1675. The country wife of the title has, like Lady Teazle, married a much older man, though Mr Pinchwife, as his name suggests, is more savagely mocked than Sir Peter. Pinchwife is an old rake being punished for marrying by having his new wife seduced by a friend – although unlike Lady Teazle, Margery Pinchwife has no qualms about actively responding to a lover. The **satire** is harsher: society is portrayed as concerned only with wit, pleasure and superficial reputations.

Sheridan uses elements of the **burlesque**, including the identification of character types by names such as Sneerwell, Backbite and Candour; Congreve makes similar use of names in *The Way of the World*, with his Petulant, Sir Wilfull Witwould and Lady Wishfort. The satiric tradition also harks back to the works of Ben Jonson at the beginning of the seventeenth century, such as *Volpone* and *The Alchemist*, in which the disorders of society are more savagely ridiculed; in Jonson's world there seem to be almost no virtuous characters and success appears to go to the most outrageous swindler. By comparison with Jonson, Sheridan seems much milder, and more hopeful that the virtuous can succeed and redeem at least those who are foolish or misguided. The comedy of manners lapsed after Sheridan's time until it was revived at the end of the nineteenth century by Oscar Wilde and George Bernard Shaw – both, like Sheridan, Irish by birth. Wilde portrays members of a sophisticated, leisured society who relish witty conversation, though there is often

CONTEXT

'Sheridan was not innovative. He did not anticipate the age which followed his own in exploring the recesses of the human personality. His characters lack subtlety of emotion and motivation. Yet he uses them with superb theatrical effect, and he gives them lines that, in concision and profundity of insight into social relationships, not infrequently recall Dryden, his favourite poet, and Pope' (Loftis, *Sheridan and the Drama of Georgian England*, p. 102).

a darker undercurrent of social commentary. In *A Woman of No Importance* (1893), Mrs Arbuthnot comments in Act IV on 'the difference between men and women': '... the ending is the ordinary ending. The woman suffers. The man goes free.'

Sheridan's satirical wit may by the end of the eighteenth century have seemed backward looking and the society he depicted doubtless soon looked out of touch with the mood of the times. Satire, however, lived on; Byron, whom Sheridan befriended in 1812, used the term 'burlesque' to describe his mock-epic poem *Don Juan* (published in parts but left incomplete at this death in 1824). Although the story concerns Don Juan's love life, it has many topical, and satirical, digressions on politics, poetry, marriage and much else besides. The novelist Jane Austen was reported to have taken the part of Mrs Candour in a reading of *The School for Scandal*. It is possible to recognise in her dialogue for the garrulous Miss Bates and the vulgar Mrs Elton in *Emma* (1816) a satirical tone that would not be out of place in Sheridan's dramas. In turn, Sheridan admired her *Pride and Prejudice* (1813) as 'one of the cleverest things he had ever read'; as Claire Tomalin comments, 'it must have reminded him of his own mastery of dialogue' (*Jane Austen: A Life*, Penguin, 1998, p. 220–1).

THEATRE IN THE LATE EIGHTEENTH CENTURY

Theatres grew in size during the eighteenth century to accommodate the larger audiences that could now afford to attend. Staging also became more sophisticated, though it would seem relatively crude by modern standards. The auditorium was lit by chandeliers, making it brighter than many private houses; because it was impractical to extinguish the candles, the audience could see each other as well as the actors throughout the play (there was also the constant danger of falling hot wax). The theatre, then, was a place to be seen as well as to see. In *The School for Scandal*, Charles comments on changes in the fashion for wigs – in a contemporary production of the play, the gentlemen would have worn their own hair, powdered white, while the women wore wigs, to reflect the fashions. Moses, however, as Zoffany's 1781 portrait indicates, wore an old-fashioned wig, long but without powder, to show that though wealthy he was not a gentleman.

? QUESTION

'English drama is a procession of glittering Irishmen: Farquhar, Goldsmith, Sheridan, Shaw, Wilde, Synge and O'Casey' (Tynan, *Theatrical Writings*). How far do you see Sheridan as an 'Irish' writer?

CONTEXT

An evening at the theatre in Sheridan's time began between 5 and 6 p.m. About two-thirds of the way through the main play, unsold seats were reduced to half-price so there was another crush of admissions – and members of the gentry often arrived late, when they had finished dinner, dismissing the servants who had been holding their seats. The main play would be followed by an after-piece (a pantomime, a **farce** or a burlesque).

In London the two Royal Patent theatres had a monopoly which they jealously guarded, and which represented a considerable investment by shareholders such as the famous actor-manager Garrick and later Sheridan himself. (The theatres, just a short distance from each other, still operate today: Covent Garden is now the Royal Opera House.) By the time Sheridan had rebuilt Drury Lane in 1794 it had become 'a wilderness of a place' in the words of the actor Mrs Siddons, where the need to enlarge their actions and make their voices heard meant a loss of subtlety for the actors. Accounts of the first production of *The School for Scandal* indicate that the cast was particularly well suited to the play – Sheridan, as a practical man of the theatre, wrote with the skills of his company in mind – and through clever casting was able to make the most of the sophisticated demands of the text.

Contemporary illustrations show that the forestage still jutted out into the auditorium, with boxes on either side close to the actors with doors next to them on both sides of the stage. There was now a deep 'scene' behind the **proscenium arch** that allowed for special effects. Garrick had brought the celebrated continental designer and painter Philip de Loutherbourg to Drury Lane in 1771, where his dramatic scenery, with cut-out effects and concealed lighting, was much admired. Normally plays would use stock scenery painted on drop cloths and flats; the importance of *The School for Scandal* for the Drury Lane management is indicated by the fact that de Loutherbourg painted two new sets for the play, one of Charles' picture gallery, complete with portraits on the walls, the other an elegant library for Joseph, with bookcases and a full-length rear window.

Scenery flats were held in grooves in the stage floor so that the acting area could be made smaller by pushing them in from each side. There could be more than one set of flats, giving additional flexibility. Painted backcloths were raised and lowered by pulleys and ropes from the flies above the stage and drop cloths could be lowered on a roller to provide further scene changes. The main curtain would rise after the prologue and not fall till the very end of the play, so that stagehands would often be seen moving furniture and scenery, though the end of an act would be indicated by

CONTEXT

The Stage Licensing Act of 1737 had two significant effects. All new plays had to be submitted for review by the Lord Chamberlain, instituting a form of censorship that lasted until 1968, and a monopoly was granted by Royal Patent to Covent Garden and Drury Lane to stage plays in London during the profitable winter season. The result was to keep political **satire** out of the theatre and discourage productions of new plays.

CHECK THE BOOK

For a painting of the theatre as it looked after Sheridan rebuilt and enlarged it in 1794 see the relevant chapter of Phyllis Hartnoll's *The Theatre: A Concise History*.

lowering a drop scene at the proscenium arch. With these details in mind it is possible to envisage how *The School for Scandal* would have looked when first staged. A manuscript **prompt book**, for example, mentions a 'drop-chamber' for the first scene in Charles' house (Act III Scene 2); this would be a backcloth of an anteroom let down on a roller. After Trip has greeted Moses and Sir Oliver, a bell rings and without the actors leaving the stage the backcloth is raised for the next scene to reveal an 'antique hall ... table covered with green cloth, two decanters of wine, plenty of glasses ... Charles, Careless and 4 gents discovered at a table, drinking.'

WWW. CHECK THE NET

For more information on London theatres, including the Theatre Royal Drury Lane, with photographs and brief histories, see **www. thisistheatre.com**

World events	Author's life	Cultural events
1749 George II on British throne since 1727		**1749** Henry Fielding, *Tom Jones*; birth of Johann Wolfgang von Goethe
1751 Death of Thomas Coram, founder of Foundling Hospital in London for abandoned children	**1751** Born in Dublin (September or October); christened 'Thos. Brinsley Sheridan' on 4 November	**1751** Tobias Smollett, *The Adventures of Peregrine Pickle*; first volumes of *L'Encyclopédie* ('An Encyclopedia, or a systematic dictionary of the sciences, arts, and crafts') published in France; William Hogarth, 'Beer Street' and 'Gin Lane'
1753 British Parliament extends citizenship to Jews		
	1754 Parents and elder brother Charles move to London, leaving Richard in Dublin	**1754** Death of Fielding
1755 Lisbon earthquake and tsunami, up to 90,000 people die		**1755** Samuel Johnson, *A Dictionary of the English Language*
1756 Seven Years' War: Britain and Prussia at war with France, Austria and Russia		**1756** Birth of Wolfgang Amadeus Mozart; Frances Abington joins the Drury Lane theatre company
1757 Bengal passes into British control		**1757** Birth of William Blake
1759 Quebec captured from the French; British Museum opens	**1759** Leaves Ireland	**1759** Adam Smith, *The Theory of Moral Sentiments*; Voltaire, *Candide*; death of George Frederick Handel
1760 Death of George II; accession of George III		
		1761 Frances Sheridan, *Memoirs of Miss Sidney Biddulph*

World events	Author's life	Cultural events
	1762 Attends Harrow School as a boarder (until 1768)	**1762** Jean-Jacques Rousseau, *Émile* and *Du Contrat Social* ('The Social Contract')
1763 Peace of Paris concludes the Seven Years' War		**1763** Frances Sheridan, *The Discovery*
	1764 Parents move to France	**1764** Death of Hogarth; Horace Walpole, *The Castle of Otranto*
	1766 Death of Frances Sheridan, Richard Brinsley Sheridan's mother	
1768 John Wilkes imprisoned for attacking King George III in print		**1768** Laurence Sterne, *A Sentimental Journey through France and Italy*
1769 James Watt patents his steam engine		
1770 Captain James Cook claims the eastern coast of New Holland (Australia) for Britain	**1770** Reunited with his sister and father in Bath	**1770** Ludwig van Beethoven and William Wordsworth born
1771 Samuel Foote's *The Maid of Bath*, a farce based on Elizabeth Linley's relations with her former fiancé Walter Long; Smollett, *The Expedition of Humphry Clinker*	**1771** Thomas Gainsborough paints Elizabeth and Mary Linley at Bath; sittings are interrupted when Elizabeth flees to France	
	1772 Escorts Elizabeth Linley to France. Duels over Elizabeth with Captain Thomas Mathews in May and July; he is badly injured in the second duel	**1772** Birth of Samuel Taylor Coleridge

World events	Author's life	Cultural events
1773 Boston Tea Party; Warren Hastings appointed first Governor-General of British India	**1773** Marries Elizabeth officially in April	**1773** Oliver Goldsmith, *She Stoops to Conquer*; Hugh Kelly, *The School for Wives*
		1774 Death of Goldsmith; Johann Wolfgang von Goethe, *The Sorrows of Young Werther*
1775 Outbreak of American Revolutionary War against British forces	**1775** *The Rivals* (January), *St Patrick's Day* (May), and *The Duenna* (November) all performed at Covent Garden. First son, Thomas, born	**1775** Jane Austen born
1776 Declaration of American Independence	**1776** Becomes manager of the Theatre Royal, Drury Lane, after buying part of David Garrick's share	**1776** Edward Gibbon, *The History of the Decline and Fall of the Roman Empire* (Volume 1); Adam Smith, *An Inquiry into … the Wealth of Nations*
	1777 *A Trip to Scarborough* (February) and *The School for Scandal* (8 May); elected a member of the Literary Club at the proposal of Samuel Johnson	
1778 Franco-American alliance. Britain declares war on France	**1778** *The Camp*	**1778** Fanny Burney, *Evelina*; death of Rousseau
1779 Britain at war with Spain	**1779** *The Critic*	**1779** Death of David Garrick
1780 Gordon Riots in London (anti-Catholic)	**1780** Elected to the House of Commons as MP for Stafford	
1782 Preliminary peace talks between Britain and the United States	**1782** Serves as Under-Secretary of State for Foreign Affairs in Lord Rockingham's brief ministry	

World events	Author's life	Cultural events
1783 Coalition of North and Charles James Fox; Treaty of Paris ends war with America and includes peace with France and Spain	**1783** Secretary to the Treasury, February to December	**1783** George Crabbe, *The Village*
1784 John Wesley ordains first Methodist ministers of religion		
	1787 Speaks in the Commons on impeachment of the former Governor-General of India, Warren Hastings	**1787** Mozart, *Don Giovanni*
1788 George III's first serious bout of insanity causes the Regency Crisis; penal colony established in Australia	**1788** Speaks for prosecution on the charge of crimes against the Begums of Oudh at the impeachment of Hastings; advises the Prince of Wales during the Regency Crisis; death of his father, Thomas Sheridan	**1788** Birth of Lord Byron; death of Gainsborough
1789 George III recovers; French Revolution: fall of the Bastille, Declaration of the Rights of Man; first cotton textiles factory in Manchester	**1789** Sheridan's portrait painted by Joshua Reynolds	**1789** William Blake, *Songs of Innocence*
1790 Death of Benjamin Franklin	**1790** Sheridan praises the French Revolution in the Commons and attacks Edmund Burke	**1790** Blake, *The Marriage of Heaven and Hell*; Burke, *Reflections on the Revolution in France*
1791 Anti-Revolutionary riots in Birmingham		**1791** Thomas Paine; *The Rights of Man*; Robert Burns, *Tam o'Shanter*; John O'Keefe, *Wild Oats*; death of Mozart

World events	Author's life	Cultural events
1792 France invaded by Continental allies; French Royal family imprisoned; September Massacres in Paris	**1792** Death of his first wife, Elizabeth	**1792** Mary Wollstonecraft; *A Vindication of the Rights of Woman*; birth of Percy Bysshe Shelley; death of Joshua Reynolds
1793 Execution of Louis XVI; France declares war on Britain; The Terror: execution of Marie Antoinette and the Girondins	**1793** Death of Mary, Elizabeth Sheridan's daughter by Lord Edward Fitzgerald	**1793** Birth of John Clare
1794 Acquittal of John Horne Tooke, Thomas Holcroft and John Thelwall of treason in Britain; Robespierre executed in France	**1794** Drury Lane reopens after rebuilding and enlarging; *The Glorious First of June* (written with James Cobb to celebrate the naval success of Lord Howe)	**1794** Ann Radcliffe, *The Mysteries of Udolpho*; Blake, *Songs of Experience*
1795 Warren Hastings acquitted; Seditious Meetings Act and Treasonable Practices Act ('Two Acts')	**1795** Marries Hester Jane Ogle ('Hecca'); press accuses Sheridan of inciting rebellion when the king's coach is stoned after he stages Otway's *Venice Preserv'd*: the play is banned for seven years	
	1796 Second son, Charles Brinsley, born	
1798 Irish Rebellion; Battle of the Nile; Nelson in command in Mediterranean	**1798** Gives evidence at trial of Irish rebel Arthur O'Connor, accused of seeking French aid for a rebellion in Ireland; O'Connor acquitted	**1798** Wordsworth and Coleridge, *Lyrical Ballads*; Thomas Malthus, *An Essay on the Principle of Population*
1799 Fall of the Directorate in France; Napoleon made First Consul	**1799** *Pizarro*	
1800 Act of Union with Ireland		**1800** Maria Edgeworth, *Castle Rackrent*

World events	Author's life	Cultural events
1801 George III refuses to assent to Catholic Emancipation; William Pitt resigns as Prime Minister		
1801–2 Peace of Amiens ends war with France for a year; war breaks out again in May 1802		**1802** Walter Scott, *Minstrelsy of the Scottish Border*
1804 Return of Pitt; Napoleon becomes Emperor		**1804** Blake tried for sedition and acquitted; writes *Jerusalem* and *Milton, a Poem*
1805 Battle of Trafalgar		**1805** Wordsworth completes his first version of *The Prelude* (not published until 1850, much revised)
1806 Death of Pitt; 'Ministry of All the Talents'	**1806** Treasurer of the Navy in the 'Ministry of All the Talents'; MP for Westminster	
1807 Britain abolishes slave trade; France invades Spain and Portugal	**1807** Loses seat at Westminster; becomes MP for Illchester, a seat controlled by the Prince of Wales	**1807** Charles Lamb, *Tales from Shakespeare*
1808 Spanish uprising; Napoleon enters Madrid as king		
1809 Battle of Corunna in Spain	**1809** Drury Lane theatre burnt to the ground	**1809** Byron, *English Bards and Scotch Reviewers*; death of Joseph Haydn
1811 George III declared mad; George, Prince of Wales' Regency begins; Luddite uprisings against the changes produced by the Industrial Revolution		**1811** Shelley expelled from Oxford; publishes *The Necessity of Atheism*

World events	Author's life	Cultural events
1812 Prime Minister Spencer Perceval assassinated; war with America; Napoleon retreats from Moscow	**1812** Loses his seat after defeat in the Stafford election; becomes friends with the young Lord Byron	**1812** Robert Browning and Charles Dickens born
		1813 Robert Southey appointed Poet Laureate; Austen, *Pride and Prejudice*
1814 Fall of Paris; Napoleon abdicates; Treaty of Ghent ends American war	**1814** Imprisoned for a short period for debt; released on intervention of Prince Regent	**1814** Austen, *Mansfield Park*; Wordsworth, *The Excursion*; Scott, *Waverley*
1815 Battle of Waterloo; Surrender of Napoleon and exile to St Helena; Corn Laws introduced		**1815** Scott, *Guy Mannering*; Anthony Trollope born
1816 Spa Fields riots against the British government	**1816** Dies on 7 July; buried in Poets' Corner, Westminster Abbey	**1816** Charlotte Brontë born; Byron leaves England for last time; Austen, *Emma*
		1817 Death of Jane Austen; *Northanger Abbey* and *Persuasion* are published posthumously in 1818

FURTHER READING

BIOGRAPHY

Linda Kelly, *Richard Brinsley Sheridan: A Life*, Sinclair-Stevenson, 1997 (Pimlico edition, 1998)

Thomas Moore, *Memoirs of the Life of the Right Honourable Richard Brinsley Sheridan*, Longman, 1825, 2 vols

Fintan O'Toole, *A Traitor's Kiss: The Life of Richard Brinsley Sheridan,* Granta Books, 1997

CRITICISM AND THEATRICAL BACKGROUND

Peter Davidson (ed.), *Sheridan: Comedies* (Casebook Series), Palgrave Macmillan, 1986

John Loftis, *Sheridan and the Drama of Georgian England*, Blackwell/Harvard University Press, 1977

Phyllis Hartnoll, *The Theatre: A Concise History*, Thames and Hudson, 1968 (third edition, 1998)

CRITICAL THEORY

These books are useful introductions to theory, though they do not contain any specific material on *The School for Scandal*:

Peter Barry, *Beginning Theory*, Manchester University Press, 1995

Jonathan Culler, *Literary Theory; A Very Short Introduction*, Oxford University Press, 1997

Rob Pope, *The English Studies Book*, Routledge, 2002

Kenneth Pickering, *Key Concepts in Drama and Performance*, Palgrave Macmillan, 2005

AUDIO RECORDING

The School for Scandal, a two-CD audio recording from EMI Classics for Pleasure (catalogue number 370 5522), produced in the 1950s, reissued in 2006

Literary terms

ambiguity the capacity of words and sentences to have double, multiple or uncertain meanings

aside when a character speaks in such a way that some or all of the other characters on stage cannot hear what is being said; or they address the audience directly. It is a device used to reveal a character's private thoughts, emotions and intentions

burlesque a work which exaggerates, demeans or mocks a serious subject or art form; in *The School for Scandal*, Sheridan's targets are scandal and **sentimental comedy**

cameo role a small part which gives the actor an opportunity to make a memorable impression by displaying their skill in character acting (from *cameo*, a smooth gemstone with a raised design of a head in profile carved on it)

caricature a portrait of someone (drawn, written or acted) with exaggerated emphasis on their most distinctive traits for comic effect

comedy of manners a form of comedy which deals with the relationships and intrigues of characters in a sophisticated society, relying for comic effect on the wit of the dialogue

denouement the final part of a plot, in which uncertainties are explained and problems and mysteries are resolved

dramatic irony when the implications of an episode or a speech are better understood by the audience than the characters

farce a comedy involving a series of ridiculously unlikely turns of events, typically including disguises, outraged husbands and wives, characters hiding on stage, etc.

irony (ironic) the humorous or sarcastic use of words to imply the opposite of what they normally mean; incongruity between what might be expected and what actually happens; the ill-timed arrival of an event that had been hoped for

parody an imitation of a work of literature or a literary style designed to ridicule the original

prompt book an annotated manuscript copy of a play kept at the side of the stage by the prompter, usually containing information on sets, props, etc.

proscenium arch arch which frames the opening between stage and audience in theatres

repartee a contest of wit, in which each speaker makes a quick reply to the other, turning the argument to his or her own advantage

satire (satirical) a type of literature in which folly, evil or topical issues are held up to scorn through ridicule, irony or exaggeration

sentimental in Sheridan's time this meant showing refined feelings or moral reflections, not the modern sense of being excessively emotional

sentimental comedy a form of drama popular in the late eighteenth and early nineteenth centuries in which the central characters are tested by a series of trials and misfortunes during which they prove their virtue and are rewarded with a happy ending

soliloquy a dramatic device which allows a character to speak directly to the audience as if thinking aloud, revealing their inner thoughts, feelings and intentions

tragedy in its original sense, a drama dealing with elevated actions and emotions and characters of high social standing in which a terrible outcome becomes inevitable as a result of an unstoppable sequence of events and a fatal flaw in the personality of the protagonist. More recently, tragedy has come to include courses of events happening to ordinary individuals that are inevitable because of social and cultural conditions or natural disasters

Author of these notes

Tom Rank has a degree in English and a Graduate Certificate in Education from Leeds University, together with a Master's in Education from the University of Manchester. After a period in Pakistan with Voluntary Service Overseas, Tom taught in England for many years, becoming a Head of English at secondary level. He is now a senior examiner and principal moderator for one of the major A Level English Literature specifications, as well as a freelance editor and consultant.

York Notes for GCSE and Key Stage 3

GCSE

Maya Angelou
I Know Why the Caged Bird Sings

Jane Austen
Pride and Prejudice

Alan Ayckbourn
Absent Friends

Elizabeth Barrett Browning
Selected Poems

Robert Bolt
A Man for All Seasons

Harold Brighouse
Hobson's Choice

Charlotte Brontë
Jane Eyre

Emily Brontë
Wuthering Heights

Brian Clark
Whose Life is it Anyway?

Robert Cormier
Heroes

Shelagh Delaney
A Taste of Honey

Charles Dickens
David Copperfield
Great Expectations
Hard Times
Oliver Twist
Selected Stories

Roddy Doyle
Paddy Clarke Ha Ha Ha

George Eliot
Silas Marner
The Mill on the Floss

Anne Frank
The Diary of a Young Girl

William Golding
Lord of the Flies

Oliver Goldsmith
She Stoops to Conquer

Willis Hall
The Long and the Short and the Tall

Thomas Hardy
Far from the Madding Crowd
The Mayor of Casterbridge
Tess of the d'Urbervilles
The Withered Arm and other Wessex Tales

L. P. Hartley
The Go-Between

Seamus Heaney
Selected Poems

Susan Hill
I'm the King of the Castle

Barry Hines
A Kestrel for a Knave

Louise Lawrence
Children of the Dust

Harper Lee
To Kill a Mockingbird

Laurie Lee
Cider with Rosie

Arthur Miller
The Crucible
A View from the Bridge

Robert O'Brien
Z for Zachariah

Frank O'Connor
My Oedipus Complex and Other Stories

George Orwell
Animal Farm

J. B. Priestley
An Inspector Calls
When We Are Married

Willy Russell
Educating Rita
Our Day Out

J. D. Salinger
The Catcher in the Rye

William Shakespeare
Henry IV Part I
Henry V
Julius Caesar
Macbeth
The Merchant of Venice
A Midsummer Night's Dream
Much Ado About Nothing
Romeo and Juliet
The Tempest
Twelfth Night

George Bernard Shaw
Pygmalion

Mary Shelley
Frankenstein

R. C. Sherriff
Journey's End

Rukshana Smith
Salt on the Snow

John Steinbeck
Of Mice and Men

Robert Louis Stevenson
Dr Jekyll and Mr Hyde

Jonathan Swift
Gulliver's Travels

Robert Swindells
Daz 4 Zoe

Mildred D. Taylor
Roll of Thunder, Hear My Cry

Mark Twain
Huckleberry Finn

James Watson
Talking in Whispers

Edith Wharton
Ethan Frome

William Wordsworth
Selected Poems

A Choice of Poets

Mystery Stories of the Nineteenth Century including The Signalman

Nineteenth Century Short Stories

Poetry of the First World War

Six Women Poets

For the AQA Anthology:

Duffy and Armitage & Pre-1914 Poetry

Heaney and Clarke & Pre-1914 Poetry

Poems from Different Cultures

Key Stage 3

William Shakespeare

Henry V
Macbeth
Much Ado About Nothing
Richard III
The Tempest

YORK NOTES ADVANCED

Margaret Atwood
Cat's Eye
The Handmaid's Tale

Jane Austen
Emma
Mansfield Park
Persuasion
Pride and Prejudice
Sense and Sensibility

William Blake
Songs of Innocence and of Experience

Charlotte Brontë
Jane Eyre
Villette

Emily Brontë
Wuthering Heights

Angela Carter
Nights at the Circus
Wise Children

Geoffrey Chaucer
The Franklin's Prologue and Tale
The Merchant's Prologue and Tale
The Miller's Prologue and Tale
The Prologue to the Canterbury Tales
The Wife of Bath's Prologue and Tale

Samuel Coleridge
Selected Poems

Joseph Conrad
Heart of Darkness

Daniel Defoe
Moll Flanders

Charles Dickens
Bleak House
Great Expectations
Hard Times

Emily Dickinson
Selected Poems

John Donne
Selected Poems

Carol Ann Duffy
Selected Poems
The World's Wife

George Eliot
Middlemarch
The Mill on the Floss

T. S. Eliot
Selected Poems
The Waste Land

F. Scott Fitzgerald
The Great Gatsby

John Ford
'Tis Pity She's a Whore

E. M. Forster
A Passage to India

Michael Frayn
Spies

Charles Frazier
Cold Mountain

Brian Friel
Making History
Translations

William Golding
The Spire

Thomas Hardy
Jude the Obscure
The Mayor of Casterbridge
The Return of the Native
Selected Poems
Tess of the d'Urbervilles

Seamus Heaney
Selected Poems from 'Opened Ground'

Nathaniel Hawthorne
The Scarlet Letter

Homer
The Iliad
The Odyssey

Aldous Huxley
Brave New World

Kazuo Ishiguro
The Remains of the Day

Ben Jonson
The Alchemist

James Joyce
Dubliners

John Keats
Selected Poems

Philip Larkin
High Windows
The Whitsun Weddings and Selected Poems

Ian McEwan
Atonement

Christopher Marlowe
Doctor Faustus
Edward II

Arthur Miller
All My Sons
Death of a Salesman

John Milton
Paradise Lost Books I & II

Toni Morrison
Beloved

George Orwell
Nineteen Eighty-Four

Sylvia Plath
Selected Poems

William Shakespeare
Antony and Cleopatra
As You Like It
Hamlet
Henry IV Part I
King Lear
Macbeth
Measure for Measure
The Merchant of Venice
A Midsummer Night's Dream
Much Ado About Nothing
Othello
Richard II
Richard III
Romeo and Juliet
The Taming of the Shrew
The Tempest
Twelfth Night
The Winter's Tale

Mary Shelley
Frankenstein

Richard Brinsley Sheridan
The School for Scandal

Bram Stoker
Dracula

Jonathan Swift
Gulliver's Travels and A Modest Proposal

Alfred Tennyson
Selected Poems

Alice Walker
The Color Purple

John Webster
The Duchess of Malfi

Oscar Wilde
The Importance of Being Earnest
A Woman of No Importance

Tennessee Williams
Cat on a Hot Tin Roof
The Glass Menagerie
A Streetcar Named Desire

Jeanette Winterson
Oranges Are Not the Only Fruit

Virginia Woolf
To the Lighthouse

William Wordsworth
The Prelude and Selected Poems

W. B. Yeats
Selected Poems